Broussard's

RESTAURANT
COOKBOOK

Broussard's
RESTAURANT
COOKBOOK

Gunter and Evelyn Preuss

PELICAN PUBLISHING COMPANY
Gretna 1996

The word "Pelican" and the depiction of a pelican are trademarks
of Pelican Publishing Company, Inc.,
and are registered in the U.S. Patent and Trademark Office.

Library of Congress Cataloging-in-Publication Data

Preuss, Gunter.
 Broussard's Restaurant cookbook / Gunter and Evelyn Preuss.
  p. cm.
 Includes index.
 ISBN 1-56554-139-1 (hardcover : alk. paper)
 1. Cookery, American—Louisiana style. 2. Cookery, Creole.
3. Cookery—Louisiana—New Orleans. 4. Broussard's Restaurant.
I. Preuss, Evelyn. II. Title.
TX715.2.L68P74 1996
641.59763—dc20   95-47827
                                                        CIP

Manufactured in the United States of America
Published by Pelican Publishing Company, Inc.
1101 Monroe Street, Gretna, Louisiana 70053

Contents

Acknowledgments

We want to thank Mimi Carbery Guste for her many hours of work in the organization, deciphering, and typing of Gunter's first-draft recipes. And Roy Guste for his work as agent and developmental editor for the book.

We also want especially to thank our two sons, Andreas and Marcus—Andreas for always supporting us in our restaurant endeavors and Marc, who through his work with us, has already made Broussard's Restaurant a two-generation Preuss tradition.

Introduction

Gunter Preuss: From Breslau to Broussard's

I was born in Breslau, Germany, in 1936. Breslau is now Polish. After World War II, as many people did, we had to leave Breslau to make a life for ourselves elsewhere. When I say *we*, I speak of my parents and myself. We left at that time because my parents did not want to become Polish citizens. My parents decided to settle in West Germany, in the city of Northeim.

I was just beginning my high school years then, and was about fourteen years old. But I was interested in seeking a livelihood in the culinary arts. So I discussed it with my parents and we all agreed that I would leave the school I was attending and begin an apprenticeship in a *fleischerei*, or butcher shop, in the city of Kassel in 1950. While doing my apprenticeship, I went to school twice a week to complete my high school education. I also enrolled in a four-year business college.

The shop where I worked was an authentic Old-World European shop where we took the beef and pork from slaughter to sausage, if that was the day's order. Four years were required for the apprenticeship program then. So I did my work, learning every day and always planning the next step in my education.

From there I went to the town of Bad Salzuflen, which is in the Teutonian Forest, and that's where I learned to be a chef.

At that point I left my family for the first time to further my education on my own in a position of apprentice to the chef. During that time, my parents decided that they themselves would go into the restaurant business. They acquired a business in Kassel, which was north of where I was apprenticing. It was 1954, the same year that I began my second apprenticeship. You see, in Germany at that time, you would have a four-year apprenticeship, after which you would determine your direction of interest and then take a job in that field. To become a chef, I was required to apprentice another three years before my education was complete. So, I apprenticed, or studied, for seven years to be allowed to enter my chosen profession as chef.

The place I chose was a hotel, which would give me more than just an education in food preparation, but also how hotels operate their food services. I stayed for three years.

After this seven years of apprenticeship one can become a "journeyman" chef, and travel to other cities and countries to work and learn about other cuisines. From Bad Salzuflen, I went to Sweden, Switzerland, France, and England to work and learn.

In 1958 in Berlin I met Evelyn. She had been born and reared in West Berlin. We were married in April 1960 in West Berlin. Then, in September of that year we emigrated to the United States.

When we came to America, we went to search out a job in Kansas City, Kansas. At that time, for a foreigner to enter and work in the United States, he or she had to have a sponsor, a person or a business, that could show that they needed the particular talents and education of the individual in that business. There had to be a permanent job for you that they would guarantee to the immigration officials.

My first guaranteed job was at a country club in Kansas City, the Carriage Club. They were my first sponsors and my first employment as a chef. From my work at the Carriage Club, I was invited to head the kitchen staff at a very exclusive club in Kansas City, the River Club.

They had only about a hundred members from all over the United States who traveled regularly to Kansas City or who owned businesses there. The club was located in a beautiful spot on a high bluff overlooking the Missouri River.

From there I went to work for Gilbert Robinson, of Houlihan's, Seaport, and many other restaurant chains' fame. At that time, all they operated was the Magic Carpet Lounge at the Kansas City airport. The old airport is practically right in the city so even people who were not traveling would drive on over to come see us.

One of the first new hotels to be built in Kansas City in a long time was the Holiday Inn, right across from the airport. Mr. Gilbert himself operated the hotel and asked me to become executive chef there, which I did.

From the Holiday Inn I was asked to become executive chef at the prestigious Mission Hills Country Club. Mission Hills is one of the most exclusive areas of the city. The members of the club were Kansas City's most influential citizens. It was during my tenure here, in 1964, that Evelyn and I had our first child, our son Andreas. Evelyn and myself both wanted to have him baptized in our country of birth, Germany. We packed ourselves up, said good-bye to Mission Hills and Kansas City, and took off for Germany. We made our way to the city of Berlin to have Andreas baptized in the old church there that was bombed out during the war. It was rebuilt as a memorial to Germany's patriots and is called Kaiser Wilhelm Gedächtnis Kirche. We remained in Berlin, Germany, for three months. But since my prospects were very good in the United States, we returned in September 1964.

We returned at first to Kansas City, where we had stored all of our furniture while we were in Germany. During our trip back to the United States, I had developed some leads for a position in Boston, so I traveled alone to Boston to follow up on them. In Boston I met with officers of the Hotel Corporation of America, which is the old Royal Sonesta organization. From them I was offered a position with the Hilton Corporation in New York. I became the executive sous chef of the Statler Hilton, across from Penn Station. Things worked out well at the Statler Hilton. I stayed there for one year in that position.

The Hilton Corporation admired the work I did, so they decided to transfer me to Washington, D.C., as the executive chef in to their hotel there, the Capital Hilton. At the Capital Hilton, I had the opportunity to oversee many, many high-up political functions and dinners. The hotel was well established and a popular place for the politicians living in Washington, even ambassadors of other countries, Cabinet members, and American presidents.

Security was most important for these functions, but once it was established for me, the FBI routine for me during such functions became second nature.

At that time there was The Gridiron Club. It was strictly for men, then. The club was formed by and for journalists, owners of newspapers, and columnists. The Gridiron Club was named for the gridiron lines on a football field. Tables were set up in the form of yardlines with the ends and sides adjoining tables: a gridiron.

The tables were always elaborately decorated. At some functions they must have had twenty or thirty thousand roses; everything was always strictly formal. The roses were arranged along the lengths of the "gridiron" tables, where six to eight hundred persons were served at a time.

The guests of honor would be the president, cabinet members, senators, congressmen, and all the foreign dignitaries from the embassies. There would be a show after dinner written and performed by the members that included satiric sketches about the guests of honor. These shows were performed on a separate stage.

The menus were traditional. The soup course was always Maryland Terrapin Turtle. I had never seen one before: a Maryland Terrapin Turtle, that is. When they came in live from Maryland, we had to corral them in the butcher shop of the hotel. It was quite a sight, 150 live turtles running around on the floor of the butcher shop.

The recipe for the turtle soup was passed from club president to club president, so we made the soup by their traditional recipe. And it was a good recipe, although our New Orleans turtle soup is measurably more delicious.

Another traditional part of the menu was corn bread sticks made from antique cast-iron baking forms that the club kept for each function. The corn bread sticks were served as the appetizer. The rest of the dinner varied between traditional and continental.

At one function where President Lyndon Johnson was the guest of honor, he sent back the chocolate mousse with the captain, who repeated the president's words exactly for me, in the president's own pronunciation, "I want some vanilla ice cream, I don't like this goddamn *mouse!*"

It was through a Swiss friend in New York that I was first introduced to the possibility of coming to New Orleans. That Swiss gentleman, Guy Frey, had been the executive steward at the Statler Hilton and had moved to New Orleans to take a position as the resident manager of the Roosevelt Hotel. In the hotel business, everybody knows everybody, so he recommended me for the position of executive chef at the Roosevelt.

The Roosevelt flew me down here to take a look. I remember that the Interstate was not completed. It was that long ago, now. We arrived at the Hotel Roosevelt, with its impressive marquee flashing in green and blue lights, the headliner in the Roosevelt's famous Blue Room: Jackie Leonard.

I remember getting out of the car, walking through the heavy, dark lobby and going directly up to my room. I immediately called Evelyn in Washington and said "There is no way. You wouldn't believe what the highway was like coming in from the airport, what lightbulbs they have here! The lobby looks like a funeral home!"

The reason for that first less-than-happy impression was that in the

Hilton hotels everything is usually new and bright. The room windows are large and modern. Here it was very different.

When I talked to Guy Frey, the resident manager, he introduced me to the general manager, who was well known in the city then; his name was Dan Mikalak. I told them that I would "go home and think about it, and I'll call you back."

They still wanted to tour me around the city while I was here. The only legitimate hotel at that time was the Jung Hotel. The Royal Orleans had just opened, but there was no Sonesta, no Hilton, none of the many hotels here today. So I thought to myself, "What would happen if they fired me? I would have no place to go. I would have moved everything down here."

I told Guy Frey I was going to stick it out with the Hilton in Washington. But, in the meantime, Evelyn had befriended Guy's wife. So they coerced Guy's wife, Ruth, into calling Evelyn. Then Guy and Dan arranged for her to come to New Orleans to see the city for herself.

So, Evelyn planned a little holiday, came to New Orleans alone, and was greeted by not only Guy and Dan, but also by the Roosevelt's public relations manager, Isabelle Monteleone.

Unlike during my stay here, Evelyn was entertained at Antoine's, Brennan's, and Galatoire's and toured around the beautiful Garden District and the charming French Quarter. She fell completely in love with the city. With Evelyn's newfound love for the city, and the considerable salary the Roosevelt offered me for the position of executive chef, my mind was changed.

When I handed in my resignation at the Statler, the general manager was concerned about my impending departure. He was an older man who had come from the stewarding side of the business so he still spent time in the kitchen. Whenever he had a problem, he came down very early in the morning and started washing dishes. He did this to get his frustration out. The problem could be with his wife, the hotel, or anything. So I remember this one morning: I asked if I could talk to him, please. I told him I would like to give notice and would be leaving in two weeks. Just as an example of how the old generation thinks, he looked at me and said, "Can we go into your office?" There he began, "They have just gold-leafed your name on this office door, and now you're gonna quit on me?" I said maybe he should call headquarters in Chicago and maybe they could come up with some more money. He was grumbling about the gold leaf and the business cards he had printed and all that. I had been with them for a year and a half and they just now were putting my name on the door! They were very slow to spend money.

But, the next day he called the president of Hilton Corporation. I must have been about twenty-four or twenty-five years old at that time. Mr. Carl Mottig, the president, said, "Gunter is the youngest chef in the company. We can't afford to give him a raise. All the old-timers are in Chicago like at the Palmer House. They don't make that much money!" So, I said I would stay until they had a replacement. Not long after that, we were packed up and on our way to New Orleans.

When I began at the Roosevelt, the original owners, the Seymour Weisses, had already sold it to Richard Swig. Mr. Weiss had been deceased some years, but Mrs. Weiss still lived in the hotel. I was there for the title change from the Roosevelt to the Fairmont-Roosevelt.

I began at the Fairmont in 1967 and remained the executive chef for three years. I then became the food and beverage manager and worked in that position until 1972.

When I first started working at the Roosevelt, we lived in the hotel for about six months. We had come from a townhouse in Fairfax, Virginia, and our younger son, Marcus, had been born in Fairfax. So we were looking for the same environment. They were building the same kind of homes in Jefferson Parish, so we waited for one to be built and we lived in the Fairmont. This was some experience!

When I started working, the family were all upstairs. I always made a big deal about the fact that my family wasn't settled. I did not want to start working until they were. We were in a new city. We had to get the kids in a home of our own. But, I began working before we were settled because we found a home that we wanted, but it was still under construction. And would be for six months more, which we certainly did not anticipate.

The Roosevelt's prior chef, a German fellow by the name of Hans Lauer, had left his sous chef at the hotel. But I learned that he was planning on leaving, as well. Soon all of Lauer's crew were gone and I needed capable people with whom I had worked before to be able to put things in order as quickly as possible.

At the time, this hotel was the biggest place in the city, room-wise as well as food and beverage-wise. There was a coffee shop on University Place; the Blue Room night club, which served meals and cocktails; the Plantation Room; the Rendezvous Room, which was the hotel restaurant; the Sazarac Bar, which served cocktails; the Fairmont Court; and room service. The hotel kitchen served four to five thousand meals a day. That's no small amount of work, believe me.

I had walked into this job completely cold, with the previous crew leaving. I immediately organized to bring as much of my staff from Washington as would come. My sous chef was Austrian and the other principal chefs were all European-trained. We all knew hard work and how to work together. But even with our solid efforts, it still took a while for this all to become well organized. But with this good staff, as chef of the Fairmont I was able to establish the quality and level of food that has become the expected high quality of Fairmont fare.

By 1970, there were new restaurants beginning to open in New Orleans. Some with great success. Evelyn and I discussed the fact that she believed that with the experience and training I had, we could be successful in a restaurant of our own. Evelyn said, "We can do it!" So we did. If it had not been for Evelyn, I never would have gone into the restaurant business.

We acquired the Versailles in 1972. Now I was back in the kitchen as chef, but for the first time, it was my *own* kitchen. The menu I created for Versailles were dishes of my own invention that took a part from European food and a part from traditional New Orleans food. The wonderful food products of this area of the country contribute greatly to what a chef can do with his imagination.

I was operating the restaurant alone, that is, without Evelyn, for a year. She had the children to care for and the house and really was too busy to spend any time there. But one day, about a year after we had opened, I had gotten an idea to freshen up the look of the dining room and covered the tables with varying colored, oilcloth tablecloths. I thought it looked nice and wanted Evelyn to come see it. She came. When Evelyn saw the cloths she told the waiters to remove them from the tables and throw them in the trash. They did what she told them. She then went home and proceeded, with the assistance of her mother, to make the tablecloths herself. From that day on, Evelyn never left the dining room.

In 1984, Broussard's came into our lives.

A former friend of ours came to us with a business opportunity. It was the purchase of Broussard's. We became partners in the purchase of the restaurant for a while, but we were very silent partners. We still spent our time Uptown at Versailles. We assisted in the operation of

Broussard's behind the scenes, improving the look of the dining rooms and the quality of the food served. But after eight years, in 1993, we bought our partner out. Now we are the sole owners of Broussard's.

I went immediately to work revising the menu and Evelyn went to work on the courtyard and the dining rooms. From the praise we have received from customers and the food critics alike, we feel that we have vastly improved the restaurant, and Broussard's is again ranked among the finest of New Orleans restaurants, a position once already held by the restaurant under the tenure of its founder and chef, Joseph Broussard.

Although serving city celebrities, the media, film stars, performers, musicians, writers, and government officials is standard operation here, there is a single individual whom we served that remains a highlight—Pope Paul XI.

The pope visited New Orleans in September of 1987. We were selected to serve the pope and his entourage at the archbishop's residence. The affair reminded me a great deal of the Gridiron functions in Washington: the ceremony, the security, and the careful checking out of each person involved.

When the meal was over, the pope himself asked for us. We were taken into a private sitting room of the residence, where he spoke with us alone and thanked us graciously for the meal we had provided. It was a very special moment for us.

We hope that each person that comes into Broussard's appreciates the decor, the service, the food, and the work that goes into providing the total dining experience. We strive to do our best and it seems that our best is working.

The year of 1995 was the seventy-fifth anniversary of the founding of Broussard's. It is for that memorable occasion that I wrote this book with my wife, Evelyn. And, also to collect for the many, many people who dine with us and compliment us by asking for our recipes, we have compiled this work.

We thank everyone who has helped us along the way and everyone who has and will in the future enjoy a meal with us at the Preuss' Broussard's Restaurant.

Evelyn Preuss

I was born, reared, and educated in Berlin, Germany. After graduating as a kindergarten teacher, I went to Zurich, Switzerland, as a governess to a prominent doctor's family. They had two children. I was hired to teach them proper German, manners, etc.—I spent all day with them.

They also had a beautiful home in Klosters, Switzerland, which is a popular ski resort. It was a very nice life I was living for those two years. The little boy was three years old and the girl five, the same difference between my own children-to-be.

But, after two years with the family, whom I had learned to love very much, it was time for me to move on with my own life. I said good-bye to my adopted family and moved back to Berlin.

In Berlin, my sister and her husband were always talking about "America." So that eventually became what I wanted to do, to go to America. My heart was soon truly set on America.

But then I met Gunter. He was a friend of my sister and her husband. My brother-in-law worked together with Gunter in a restaurant in Berlin. He came by one day to visit my brother-in-law, and when I opened the door he was interested in me. He asked my sister if he could please ask me to go out with him. She right away said, "I don't think she will."

But Gunter was not going away that easily and he persisted in asking if I would go out with him. Well, I finally did go out with him and a year later we were engaged.

From the very beginning of our relationship I kept telling Gunter that we had to go to America, maybe for only two years or so. He was totally against it. But I was as persistent as he had been about asking me to go out with him and we left for America in 1960.

America here we come! My sister and brother-in-law were now living and working in Kansas City. They found an apartment for us and Gunter got a job where my brother-in-law worked.

Here I was home all day in an apartment that people seemed endlessly coming and going, knocking on the door all day wanting to bring me coffee and cookies. All I really wanted to be was alone. After finally getting to America, I realized it was not the place I had dreamed it would be. I began crying and crying and seemed to never stop. I played music all day so no one would hear me and locked myself in the apartment. I wanted to go home to Germany.

We did not go home to Germany, but instead we moved on to

better and better positions. The next place was really nice and I made up my mind to get better or get out. So I got myself together and bought a car. Gunter did not drive, so I took him back and forth to work every day. Things were becoming very nice. I concentrated on decorating our apartment. It was so pretty; it looked like a little palace.

By this time we had made some very good friends. I must say, when you're just starting out and you don't have anything, good friends are the most important thing you can have. We gave a lot of parties and were really beginning to feel at home in America.

One day a German friend came to one of our parties. He was working at one of Kansas City's best restaurants. He said, "Evelyn, they are looking for a hostess for the restaurant. Why don't you apply?" I said, "With my little bit of English? No chance!" But I applied anyway and, don't you know, I got the job.

My job as hostess basically was to take customers to their tables and with my few words of English say, "Have a nice meal." If they asked me anything at all I would have to turn around and find help to answer them. Everybody was so nice; I was not used to that having come from a big city like Berlin.

After four years I had my always-wanted baby, Andreas. I left my job and stayed home to take care of the family and home. We traveled to New York and then to Washington, D.C., where Gunter worked in different hotels. But I always wished that one day we would have our own beautiful restaurant. As our homes got better and better as we moved around, so did our life-style. Our second son, Marcus, was born and I was so happy raising the two boys. I did lots of working, gardening, and enjoyed just being a mom. Gunter was very happy, too—until the call came from New Orleans. "What a good deal!" I told him. "Let's go!" Well, you know the story from Gunter.

We lived and worked here in New Orleans for about five years. Then, at a party one night, sincerely now my best friend here, Marta, told us of a restaurant that had recently closed and the space was available. My ears picked up and I couldn't wait to tell Gunter. We went immediately to see the space and fell in love with it. Soon we were the proud owners of the Versailles Restaurant.

Gunter was both chef and operator of the restaurant. For the first year, the boys were still little so I had to say at home to care for them. Gunter was handling the business alone, until one day.

Gunter proudly announced to me that he had found great tablecloths and that I should come by and see how they improved the look of the dining room. Well, I drove by the restaurant and from my car on Saint Charles Avenue I could see them. They were many colors and made of some oilcloth or plastic. I said, "That's it." I went into the restaurant and had the help throw the cloths in the trash. My mother and myself sat down and made beautiful new cloths for the restaurant. From that day on I never left.

Many other things changed after that. I redecorated the restaurant to be elegant and stayed in the dining room to talk to the customers and make them feel at home. But it felt like I was born to do so. There was a great deal to do. I loved it.

The hardest thing was leaving the boys to come to work, working on the weekends. But there was always a hot meal on the table before I left them to go to work; they were well taken care of. Marc, my youngest, was so upset with my working. When I would try to leave for the evening, he would fight with me, holding on to me, until we were both totally wrecked. Gunter would call home to ask where I was and to tell me that the customers were all asking for me. I would arrive at the restaurant with my hair askew, sometimes my skirts even torn. Then I would quickly get myself together, to look the way a hostess should, to greet the customers.

Now, twenty-five years later, the boys are very proud of their mom. I am now involved in our two restaurants and continue to use all of my interests in interior design, public relations, and most of all, people.

I have my two sons, Andreas and Marcus, and a loving husband, Gunter, who lets me be me. *My dreams have come true.*

Broussard's Restaurant: Joseph C. Broussard

For many years, more than three-quarters of a century, New Orleanians have enjoyed the continued existence and culinary dominance of a mere handful of great restaurants: four to be exact. These restaurants are Antoine's, Arnaud's, Galatoire's, and Broussard's. Their founding dates ranged from 1840 to 1920, and their continued existence is testament to their excellence and leadership in the New Orleans culinary world.

That is certainly not to say that there have not been many other smaller neighborhood establishments of considerable recognition, but it is this group that has carried the torch of culinary excellence for generations here in the Crescent City, as New Orleans is known. Broussard's is also one of the restaurants primarily responsible for New Orleans' worldwide reputation as a culinary capital.

The job done by the operators of these restaurants has been rather remarkable. They remain remarkable today in the excellence of repasts that continue to flow from their grand kitchens to the many thousands of diners who continue to enjoy their dining experiences.

In 1920, the doors of Broussard's Restaurant opened. It was Joseph C. Broussard, accompanied by his young wife, Rosalie Borrello, and his brother Robert, who began the restaurant.

Joseph Broussard was born in Loreauville, Evangeline Parish, Louisiana. As a young man he was always interested in good food and the pleasure of enjoying meals with friends and family. He knew at a young age that he would one day open his own restaurant. But he also knew that it would be to New Orleans, the Paris of the Americas, that he must go to learn his craft and build his business.

It was in 1902 that Broussard arrived in New Orleans to pursue his dream of opening and operating his own restaurant. Antoine's being the grandest restaurant in the city, that was the place where young Broussard sought his employment.

At Antoine's he presented himself to Jules Alciatore, son of Antoine Alciatore and second-generation proprietor, to interview for a job at the restaurant. Jules was impressed by the demeanor of young Broussard and employed him as an assistant waiter. Although Broussard was inclined toward employment in the kitchen, he accepted the position knowing that he must learn the service of dining as well as the preparation of food to one day become a proprietor himself. In this position he learned the fine points of service in an establishment that catered to the aristocracy of the city, as well as to wealthy, continental travelers who expected and demanded only the finest in food and service. Broussard was as astute as he was dedicated: he learned quickly.

Soon his progress had brought him to such a level of expertise in service that Jules advanced him from assistant waiter to waiter, a position traditionally reserved for employees who had spent at least several years' service at the restaurant. Broussard was happy with

Jules' confidence and offer, so, although his desire to enter the kitchen staff persisted, he knew it would be best for him to follow the path that Jules was now laying out for him.

After two years as a waiter, after having met and served all of Antoine's regular customers, after having his excellence of service brought to Jules' attention by the customers on a daily basis, Joseph approached Mr. Alciatore with the request that he enter service in the kitchen. Jules was reluctant to lose the fine abilities of this conscientious young man in the dining room, but knew now of Broussard's dream and allowed the transition.

In the kitchen at Antoine's, he was sent to the bottom rung of the staff, accepted the considerable decrease in salary that he had earned as waiter, and began to learn the cuisine served at Antoine's. His familial knowledge of Louisiana fare was well developed. So with this base, he began to learn and decipher the influences that determined Louisiana cuisine and the differences in them. He had the good fortune of not only having attracted Jules' attention to his abilities as waiter, but now found himself working under New Orleans' most capable chefs.

Jules Alciatore had himself mastered the arts of both Louisiana and French cuisines and had became a true artist in the kitchen. Broussard became an astute student of Jules and worked hard to learn and to assist as much as he could. Because Broussard was willing to accept extra work in the kitchen aside from his daily duties in food preparation, Jules would bring him close to his side when he felt there was something important being performed for Broussard to learn. And learn he did.

During these years of service Broussard lived a frugal existence outside of his work. While many of his young co-workers were living the "good life" that the city had to offer, he saved his earnings, as much as he possibly could, toward realizing his dreams.

It was not long before Broussard had acquired the knowledge of the preparation of all of Antoine's many dishes and had exhausted the knowledge that he could acquire from a single kitchen. It was time to move on.

Broussard approached Jules concerning the acquisition of a letter of recommendation and introduction that he could carry with him to Paris, where he hoped to spend time in a true French kitchen. Jules was sorry to have such a capable employee leave the restaurant, but he well understood the desire of the young man to be his own master. To that end, Jules did more than equip Broussard with a letter of recommendation. He actually brought him to Paris.

It was the custom of the Alciatores to close the doors of Antoine's every summer for several months, when the heat and fevers made life unbearable. He would travel to Europe as vacation for the family, but also as learning tour for himself to see and experience firsthand what the chefs of Europe were creating anew in their restaurants. Jules invited young Broussard to join them in their journey to Paris, and then to assist him in finding a position.

Jules had written ahead to Mornay Voiron, chef of Restaurant Durand—one of the great restaurants of Paris at the time, to arrange an interview between Voiron and Broussard. Broussard's Louisiana French language enabled him to speak fluently with the famed chef. After his favorable interview and Jules' recommendation, Broussard was hired as a chef's assistant in Voiron's kitchen. In those days, the chefs' assistants were paid little for their work because it was considered a training education. The student's parents usually paid the chef, just as they would have paid a university to allow him to study an arts or business curriculum. The custom still survives today in the great restaurants of France. So for Broussard, it was good that he had been as prudent as he had been with his financial affairs in New Orleans.

The Restaurant Durand was one of Paris' best, with a history as colorful as existed. In the 1860s, with the advent of the Civil War in America, Paris was a brisk and sparkling city. At that time, Durand was considered one of the three great restaurants of the city, along with the Cafe Riche and the Cafe Hardy. Durand was named for Charles Durand, born in Provence, and called the Carême de la Cuisine Provençale. Durand is credited with popularizing Provençal cuisine throughout France. After his death in 1854, his huge popularity was reason for the operators of this Place Madeleine temple of cuisine to be named Durand.

Such luminaries as Alexandre Dumas, Anatole France, Boulangere and Emile Zola—who actually sat at a table in Durand and wrote his famous work J'Accuse—frequented the dining rooms of the restaurant. It was in this restaurant, in the latter part of the nineteenth century that the restaurant's chef, the renowned Voiron, invented the ubiquitous Sauce Mornay, naming it for his son and sous chef, Mornay Voiron. It was Mornay who was at the "piano," as the principal stove of the restaurant was known, at the time of Broussard's apprenticeship in Paris.

Broussard was now being introduced to highest level of classic French cuisine, as well as the much loved cuisine Provençale. Broussard remained in the kitchen of Durand, and learned what he could during that time, always asking questions and studying books that Voiron would allow him to read in the little time he had late at night before he slept.

But as a student, earning no money, his funds were eventually exhausted. He left Paris and returned to New Orleans before his nest egg of saved funds was completely exhausted.

Returning to New Orleans, Broussard set about to make plans for his restaurant. He was employed as a chef in various restaurants in the city, again saving his earnings toward the end of opening his own. He soon met young Rosalie Borrello. His dream aside, Joseph fell in love with the lovely Rosalie and asked for her hand in marriage. Her parents were pleased with the union, as well as with Joseph's ambitions. They were so pleased, in fact, that as a wedding gift, Rosalie's parents gave the young couple a building on Conti Street, Rosalie's girlhood home, as a place where the couple could both live and open their restaurant.

Things were now in place. Joseph's training was complete and now, through the generosity of his father-in-law, he had not only the wife he loved but also a building for their restaurant.

It would be 1920 when Broussard finally achieved his dream and the doors of his restaurant opened.

Broussard made his mark among the finest restaurants in New Orleans. He served up expert renditions of both Creole and Parisian fare. He incorporated the courtyard behind the property into the restaurant area, naming it after Napoleon. Dining in the Napoleon Courtyard became an immediate success of Broussard's as well as did his particular service of the famed Napoleon cognac. When Napoleon cognac was ordered, a great bell was rung and the waiters sang "La Marseillaise" as they marched the cognac to the table. But the bell stopped ringing in 1966 when Joseph died. New Orleans mourned the passing of one of its culinary greats at a Requiem High Mass in Saint Louis Cathedral.

His descendants carried on the operation of the restaurant for a while, but their interests lay elsewhere. Broussard's eventually closed it doors.

In 1974, the property was purchased by restaurateurs Joseph Marcello and his nephew Joseph C. Marcello. Under their ownership the restaurant underwent a major renovation and was reopened in 1975. The Marcellos operated the restaurant several years before selling it to new owners, including Gunter and Evelyn Preuss. The Preusses eventually acquired full ownership and are now sole proprietors of Broussard's Restaurant.

The Property

The oldest building of the restaurant complex is that now occupied by the Magnolia Room. It was originally built in the 1830s as the stables for the Hermann and Grima families' home on Saint Louis Street. At that time, the Hermann-Grima property ran through the entire center of the block from Saint Louis to Conti Street.

The restaurant restoration of the stable building "uncovered exceptionally fine examples of construction and design techniques substantially preserving the original fabric." This statement was made by the architectural historians of The Vieux Carré Commission for the Vieux Carré Survey, which rates in order of historical importance the existing Vieux Carré buildings. This building rated among the highest.

The building now occupied by the Josephine Room was built pre-1876, and originally used as washroom for the Hermann-Grima home. A small Creole cottage once occupied the area now fronting Conti Street.

The buildings on this property from 1835 to 1885 were occupied by the Jefferson Academy, a leading boys' academy that specialized from the primary grade to the completion of the academic course in a curriculum of English, French, writing, mathematics, geography, history, bookkeeping, and fencing. Fencing was once a necessary part of a boy's proper training in New Orleans.

The ravages of time caused the front Conti Street cottage to be razed to make room for the present building, that which you enter as the present-day Broussard's. The remainder of the buildings on the present property were built between 1900 and 1929.

The courtyard also boasts the growth of the oldest and largest Wisteria in the French Quarter.

ABBREVIATIONS

STANDARD

tsp.	=	teaspoon
tbsp.	=	tablespoon
oz.	=	ounce
qt.	=	quart
lb.	=	pound

METRIC

ml.	=	milliliter
l.	=	liter
g.	=	gram
kg.	=	kilogram
mg.	=	milligram

STANDARD-METRIC APPROXIMATIONS

⅛ teaspoon	=	.6 milliliter		
¼ teaspoon	=	1.2 milliliters		
½ teaspoon	=	2.5 milliliters		
1 teaspoon	=	5 milliliters		
1 tablespoon	=	15 milliliters		
4 tablespoons	=	¼ cup	=	60 milliliters
8 tablespoons	=	½ cup	=	118 milliliters
16 tablespoons	=	1 cup	=	236 milliliters
2 cups	=	473 milliliters		
2½ cups	=	563 milliliters		
4 cups	=	946 milliliters		
1 quart	=	4 cups	=	.94 liter

SOLID MEASUREMENTS

½ ounce	=	15 grams		
1 ounce	=	25 grams		
4 ounces	=	110 grams		
16 ounces	=	1 pound	=	454 grams

Broussard's
RESTAURANT
COOKBOOK

Appetizers

CRABMEAT BROUSSARD

1 tbsp. butter
6 jumbo shrimp, peeled, tail
    left on, deveined; butterfly
1 oz. (2 tbsp.) olive oil
1 small yellow onion, diced
2 fresh artichoke hearts,
    chopped
1 large clove garlic, minced
¼ cup flour

¼ cup white wine
2 cups chicken stock
1 cup heavy cream
3 oz. brie cheese
½ cup bread crumbs
3 tbsp. olive oil
1 tbsp. whole fresh thyme
    leaves
¾ lb. jumbo lump crabmeat

Preheat the oven to 400 degrees.

In a large skillet, melt the butter and sauté the shrimp until they are just cooked. Set aside to cool.

In a heavy saucepan, heat the olive oil and sauté the yellow onion, artichoke hearts, and garlic over medium heat until the onion becomes limp. Sprinkle in the flour and mix well while cooking for a minute more. Deglaze the pan with the white wine, then add stock. Bring to a boil, reduce heat, and simmer for three minutes.

Add the heavy cream and simmer for another five minutes. Remove the saucepan from the heat and let stand for about three minutes.

Take the brie and scrape off and discard the white skin; cut cheese into small pieces. Add brie to the cream sauce and stir until all of the cheese is melted and mixed well. Remove from heat and allow to cool.

In a small bowl, combine the bread crumbs, olive oil, and thyme. Set aside.

After the cheese mixture is cool, gently fold in the crabmeat, being careful not to break up the lumps.

To assemble, place one shrimp in the center of an ovenproof serving dish so that it stands. Spoon the crabmeat mixture around the shrimp and sprinkle with the bread-crumb mixture. Repeat with the remaining shrimp.

Arrange the dishes on a large baking pan and bake in the preheated oven for fifteen minutes, or until the crab mixture is hot and bubbly. Serve immediately. *Serves 6.*

Note: This dish was served to Steven Segal on a "film" visit to New Orleans.

CRABMEAT TERRINE

1 lb. salmon or trout fillets
2 tbsp. chopped green onion
¼ tsp. white pepper
¼ tsp. black pepper
¼ tsp. cayenne pepper
¾ tsp. salt
2 tbsp. lemon juice
2 tbsp. white wine

1 bay leaf
¼ tsp. minced garlic
½ cup egg whites
½ cup heavy cream
½ lb. jumbo lump crabmeat
Crab fingers for garnish
Parsley, small bunch
   for garnish

Cut fish fillets crosswise into 1-inch pieces and place them in a pan or container. Combine the chopped green onion, white, black, and cayenne peppers, salt, lemon juice, white wine, bay leaf, and minced garlic. Cover the fish fillet pieces with this mixture, cover the container, and refrigerate to marinate overnight.

The next day, preheat the oven to 325 degrees. In a food processor, puree the fish fillets and the marinating mixture until very smooth. Add the egg whites in three stages, allowing each addition to mix well before adding the next. Now, add the cream gradually.

Transfer the mixture to a bowl and fold in the crabmeat gently.

When thoroughly combined, put the mixture into a 1- to 1½-quart loaf pan. Place this pan in another pan of hot water at least halfway up the side. Bake in the preheated oven for 1 hour and 15 minutes. A cake tester will come out clean when done. Allow to rest 15 minutes, unmold, and refrigerate. Serve slices decorated with crab fingers and fresh parsley sprigs. *Makes 1 quart.*

CRABMEAT RAVIGOTE

1½ lb. jumbo lump crabmeat
1 cup Ravigote Sauce
3 ripe avocados
3½ cups water
¼ cup fresh lemon juice

3 cups chopped Boston lettuce
1 cup chopped radicchio
6 tsp. capers
6 lemon slices

Gently fold the crabmeat into the Ravigote Sauce, cover, and refrigerate overnight.

Peel and halve the avocados; discard the pits. Mix the water and lemon juice and soak the avocados for about 2 hours. This will make it possible to prepare the dish early and the avocados will not discolor.

Combine the Boston lettuce and radicchio and divide it onto 6 chilled plates. Place an avocado half in the center of the lettuce and fill with the crabmeat mixture. Sprinkle with the capers and garnish with a slice of lemon. *Serves 6.*

CRABMEAT VERSAILLES

2 tbsp. fresh butter
1 tsp. sliced green onions
1 tsp. minced dry shallots
¼ tsp. minced garlic
½ cup white wine
Juice from ¼ lemon
1¾ cups medium-thick
  Béchamel Sauce

1 tbsp. fresh dill
1½ lb. jumbo lump crabmeat
Salt to taste
Pinch cayenne pepper
½ cup freshly grated Parmesan
  cheese
3 lemons halved, for garnish
6 fresh dill sprigs, for garnish

Preheat the oven to 350 degrees.

In a sauté pan or saucepan, melt the butter and sauté the green onions, shallots, and garlic for 2 minutes without browning.

Add the white wine and lemon juice and reduce by half.

Add the Béchamel Sauce and dill and reduce by another third. Add the lump crabmeat, season to taste with salt and cayenne pepper, and simmer for 10 minutes more.

To serve, spoon the Crabmeat Versailles into six ramekins or small seashells, sprinkle with the freshly grated Parmesan cheese, and bake in the preheated oven until the cheese is golden and the sauce is bubbly. Garnish each serving with half of a lemon and a sprig of dill. *Serves 6.*

ARTICHOKES WITH CRABMEAT

Enough water to cover six artichokes	**6 medium artichokes, trimmed and hollowed**
3 lemons, halved	**2 cups Crabmeat Florentine**
1 tbsp. salt	**1½ cups Béarnaise Sauce**

In enough water to cover the artichokes, squeeze the juice from the three halved lemons, add the lemons themselves, and the salt. Bring to a boil, add the artichokes and cook for 45 minutes, or until done. Drain the artichokes and keep them warm.

Put each artichoke in a small casserole that will hold it upright. Fill each cavity with the Crabmeat Florentine mixture and nap the top with Béarnaise Sauce. Glaze under a broiler and serve. *Serves 6.*

LOUISIANA CRABCAKES WITH CREOLE MUSTARD-CAPER SAUCE

1½ lb. jumbo lump crabmeat	**½ tsp. dry mustard**
½ cup sliced green onions	**1 tsp. salt**
2 tbsp. finely diced red bell pepper	**½ tsp. white pepper**
	¾ cup Béchamel Sauce
2 tbsp. finely diced yellow bell pepper	**Bread crumbs to coat crabcakes**
	½ cup vegetable oil
1½ cups bread crumbs	**Creole Mustard-Caper Sauce**

In large bowl gently toss the crabmeat with the green onions and bell peppers. Mix the bread crumbs, dry mustard, salt, and pepper together and gently fold into the crabmeat mixture. Fold in the

Béchamel Sauce gently, to avoid breaking up the crabmeat lumps.

Divide the mixture into twelve equal portions. Using your hands, press and shape each portion into a flat, round "cake." Dredge the crabcakes in the additional bread crumbs to coat. Sauté the crabcakes in the vegetable oil on both sides until golden on the outside and done on the inside. Serve with the Creole Mustard-Caper Sauce. *Serves 6, allowing 2 crabcakes each.*

Note: This recipe can also be used in the preparation of Shrimp Lafayette.

STUFFED EGGPLANT BAYOU TECHE WITH WARM REMOULADE SAUCE

2 cups Crabmeat Stuffing
12 eggplant rounds, each 1½ inches thick
1 dozen 10-15 count shrimp, peeled
Salt to taste
Black pepper to taste
Cayenne pepper to taste
Paprika to taste

1 cup flour
Eggwash of 1 whole egg and ¼ cup milk
Bread crumbs
1 cup yellow corn flour
6 green onion tops, 3 inches long
1½ cups Warm Remoulade Sauce

Heat the Crabmeat Stuffing and keep hot. Lightly sprinkle the eggplant rounds and shrimp with salt, black pepper, cayenne, and paprika. Dredge in white flour and dip in the eggwash. Roll the eggplant in the bread crumbs and shrimp in the yellow corn flour. Deep fry.

Place one slice of eggplant on a heated serving plate and spoon on the hot crabmeat stuffing. Top with one fried shrimp and then a second eggplant slice. Place a second shrimp on top and finish with a green onion top. Spoon the Warm Remoulade Sauce on top. *Serves 6.*

Note: This was a hot item for the Pan-American Culinary Olympics in New Orleans, for which I was the chef in charge.

PAN-FRIED EGGPLANT TOPPED WITH LUMP CRABMEAT, CREOLE TOMATO SAUCE, AND BASIL HOLLANDAISE

CRABMEAT TOPPING

2 tbsp. butter
2 tbsp. chopped green onions
½ tsp. chopped French shallots
½ tsp. chopped garlic
½ cup brandy

¾ lb. lump crabmeat
Salt to taste
White pepper to taste
Dash "liquid crab boil"

To prepare the crabmeat topping, heat skillet and add the butter with the green onions, shallots, and garlic. Sauté, but do not brown. Add brandy and allow to reduce slightly. Add crabmeat, season with salt and pepper, add a dash of the "liquid crab boil," and toss gently until well heated. Keep hot.

¼ cup olive oil
6½-inch thick, 2½-inch wide
    slices skinned eggplant
Salt to taste
White pepper to taste
1 cup flour
2 eggs, beaten

1 cup cornmeal
2½ cups Creole Tomato Sauce
1 tbsp. fresh butter
1 cup Basil Hollandaise
Fresh green and opal basil
    leaves for garnish

To prepare the eggplant, heat the olive oil in a skillet. Lightly salt and pepper the eggplant slices and dredge them in the flour, shaking off any excess. Immerse the slices in the beaten eggs and dredge them in the cornmeal. Pan-fry the eggplant slices in the olive oil to a golden brown on each side. Remove them to paper towels or napkins to drain. Keep warm.

To assemble the dish, heat the Creole Tomato Sauce to a simmer and add the fresh butter.

On heated plates, place an eggplant slice in the middle and top with the crabmeat mixture in a dome shape. Surround the crabmeat with a ribbon of tomato sauce and top the dome with Basil Hollandaise. Garnish with fresh green and opal basil leaves and serve. *Serves 6.*

Note: Most any crabmeat can be used. However, the idea is to avoid too much handling, which would cause the lumps to break up and become shredded and stringy.

"Liquid crab boil" is the same flavor infusion as the mixture of dried spices and herbs (mustard seed, bay leaf, thyme, etc.) used to flavor boiled seafood in Louisiana. Just a dash! It goes a long way!

CRAB BOUDIN
WITH GREEN PEPPERCORN SAUCE

2 lb. claw crabmeat, picked of
  shell pieces
1 lb. redfish fillet pieces,
  skinned
½ lb. butter (2 sticks)
3 large eggs
1 cup chopped green onions
½ cup minced parsley

3 tbsp. minced garlic
2 tbsp. lemon juice
1 tbsp. salt
1 tsp. cayenne pepper
Sausage casings
Enough salted water or fish
  stock to poach boudin
3 cups Green Peppercorn Sauce

Combine the crabmeat, redfish fillet pieces, butter, and eggs in a food processor container. Process to a smooth "dough" consistency.

Transfer the mixture to a bowl and fold in the green onions, parsley, garlic, and lemon juice. Season with the salt and cayenne pepper. Using a pastry bag or a sausage stuffing attachment to your mixer, stuff the mixture into sausage casings and tie at every 6 inches.

To cook, bring some lightly salted water or fish stock to a boil and poach the boudin to an internal temperature of 140 degrees, or simmer for 15 minutes. Serve hot with the Green Peppercorn Sauce. *Makes approximately 12-16 pieces, or 6-8 servings.*

SHRIMP AND CRABMEAT CHEESECAKE IMPERIAL WITH ROASTED RED PEPPER AND DILL CREAM

2 cups mayonnaise
2 cups sour cream
¼ cup freshly squeezed lemon juice
½ cup Dijon mustard
¼ cup chopped fresh dill
2 tsp. dried tarragon leaves, soaked in white wine for an hour and drained
2 tsp. minced roasted garlic

1 cup chopped green onions
2 tsp. paprika
¾ lb. cooked shrimp, peeled, deveined and chopped
½ cup plus 2 tbsp. cider vinegar
½ cup granulated unflavored gelatin
¼ lb. backfin lump crabmeat
Roasted Red Pepper and Dill Cream

In a large mixing bowl, combine the mayonnaise and sour cream with the freshly squeezed lemon juice, Dijon mustard, dill, drained tarragon leaves, garlic, onions, and paprika. Mix well until all ingredients are well incorporated, then fold in the chopped shrimp.

In a small sauté pan, combine the cider vinegar and gelatin, place over a moderate heat, and stir constantly until the gelatin granules are completely dissolved. Add the gelatin and vinegar mixture slowly to the other ingredients and mix well as you go.

Now, quickly but gently fold the lump crabmeat into the mixture. Be sure that it is well distributed but don't work it so much that you break up the lumps.

Pour the mixture into an 8-inch springform pan, cover with plastic wrap, and refrigerate overnight.

PECAN MIXTURE

2 tbsp. butter
1 cup pecan pieces
½ tsp. salt

¹⁄₁₆ tsp. cayenne pepper
1 tsp. Worcestershire sauce

In a sauté pan, melt the butter and add the pecan pieces, salt, cayenne pepper, and Worcestershire sauce. Sauté for 2-3 minutes until the pecan pieces are nicely browned, but not overly so. Cool the pecan mixture and rough chop. Don't refrigerate before pressing into the sides of the cake.

To complete the assembly of the cake, remove it from the springform pan and place it on a plate. Spread the Roasted Red Pepper and Dill Cream evenly over the top. Garnish the sides of the cake with the Pecan Mixture, pressing it into an even layer around the sides. Refrigerate the cake until it is ready to be served. *Makes 1 8-inch springform pan cheesecake, 15 servings.*

SHRIMP LAFAYETTE

1½ dozen large 10-15 count
   shrimp
Salt to taste
Black Pepper to taste
2 cups crabcake recipe mixture
   (from Louisiana Crabcakes

with Creole Mustard-Caper
   Sauce), final cooking not yet
   done
Oil
1¼ cups Creole Mustard-Caper
   Sauce

Preheat the oven to 400 degrees.

Peel and devein the shrimp, but don't remove the tails. Butterfly them with a deep cut so that they may stand in the baking pan. Sprinkle them lightly with salt and pepper.

Divide the crabcake mixture into eighteen portions and roll them into balls in your hands. Place a ball on each shrimp and fold the tail over the top to cover the crabcake mixture. Place the prepared shrimp in a well-oiled baking pan and bake in the preheated oven for 5 minutes.

Serve with the Creole Mustard-Caper Sauce spooned onto the plate beside each serving of three shrimp. *Serves 6.*

SHRIMP WITH TWO REMOULADES

4 qt. water
¼ cup "liquid crab boil"
¾ cup salt
3 lemons, quartered
2 lb. whole fresh shrimp
1½ cups Red Remoulade Sauce

1½ cups Green Remoulade
  Sauce
3 cups chopped Boston lettuce*
1 cup chopped radicchio*
6 lemon wedges

In a large pot combine the water with the "liquid crab boil," salt, and quartered lemons. Simmer for about 15 minutes. Add the whole shrimp and return to boil. Turn off heat and let shrimp sit for about 10-15 minutes or until they are cooked. Remove them from the water and let them cool to room temperature. Then peel and devein shrimp and chill.

Mix half of the shrimp with the Red Remoulade Sauce and half with the Green Remoulade Sauce. Refrigerate overnight.

Combine the lettuce and radicchio and divide onto 6 chilled salad plates. Place one lettuce "cup" and one radicchio "cup" on top of the chopped lettuce and radicchio and fill each with one of the two remoulades. Garnish with lemon wedges and serve. *Serves 6.*

*Reserve 6 small inner leaves from the Boston lettuce and 6 from the radicchio to use as "cups" to hold the remoulades.

CRAWFISH VERSAILLES

2 tbsp. fresh butter
2 tbsp. sliced green onions
1 tbsp. minced French shallots
2 tsp. minced garlic
½ cup white wine
Lemon juice, from ¼ lemon
1¾ cups medium-thick
  Béchamel Sauce
1½ tbsp. fresh dill, or 1½ tsp.
  dried

1½ lb. parboiled crawfish tail
  meat
Salt to taste
Pinch cayenne pepper
½ cup freshly grated Parmesan
  cheese
6 boiled crawfish for garnish

Preheat the oven to 350 degrees.

Melt the butter in a sauté or saucepan and sauté the green onions, shallots, and garlic for 2 minutes without browning.

Add the white wine and lemon juice and reduce by half. Add the Béchamel Sauce and dill and reduce by another third. Then add the crawfish tails and simmer 10 minutes. Season to taste with salt and cayenne pepper.

To serve, put the mixture in ramekins or small seashells, sprinkle with the freshly grated Parmesan cheese, and bake in the preheated oven until the cheese is golden brown and the sauce is bubbly. Garnish with a boiled crawfish and serve. *Serves 6.*

Note: We served this dish to the pope on his visit to New Orleans.

OYSTERS BROUSSARD

¼ lb. butter (1 stick)
½ lb. yellow onion, diced
½ lb. red bell peppers, seeded and diced
½ lb. green bell peppers, seeded and diced
1 lb. zucchini, sliced
1 lb. eggplant, skinned and diced
1 lb. fresh mushrooms, sliced
½ cup flour

1 cup white wine
2 qt. tomato puree
1 lb. sugar
1½ tsp. dry oregano
Salt to taste
1 tsp. white pepper
1½ tsp. Worcestershire sauce
¼ tsp. Tabasco sauce
6 bay leaves
36 oysters on the half-shell

Melt the butter in large saucepan. Add the onion and bell peppers and sauté for 5 minutes. Next add the zucchini, eggplant, and mushrooms and sauté for another 5 minutes, or until the zucchini is soft but not the consistency of a puree. Add the flour, mix well, and cook for 1 minute. Deglaze the pan with the white wine.

Next, add the tomato puree, sugar, oregano, salt, pepper, Worcestershire, and Tabasco. Mix well, add the bay leaves, and simmer until thick, about 30 minutes. The mixture should mound on a spoon. Refrigerate in a covered container until ready for use.

To bake, preheat the oven to 325 degrees. Put the fresh raw oysters on their half-shells and spoon on the cold sauce. Bake in the preheated oven for 20 minutes, or until the sauce is browned and bubbly. *Serves 6.*

OYSTERS ROCKEFELLER

2 strips bacon, minced
½ lb. celery ribs, minced
1 whole bunch parsley, minced
½ cup chopped yellow onion
1 small clove garlic, minced
Pinch ground nutmeg
1 lb. spinach, finely chopped
½ cup flour

1 tbsp. Herbsaint or Pernod
½ cup heavy cream
1 tsp. Worcestershire sauce
Salt to taste
½ tsp. white pepper
36 oysters on the half-shell
½ cup grated Parmesan cheese

In a heavy saucepan, sauté the minced bacon until crisp. Add the celery, parsley, onion, garlic, and nutmeg. Sauté for 4 minutes. Add the spinach and sauté for another 8 minutes.

Add the flour and mix well. Cook together for 1 minute more, then deglaze the pan with the Herbsaint or Pernod. Blend in the heavy cream and Worcestershire sauce. Season with the salt and pepper, bring to a boil, reduce until the sauce can mound on a spoon, and remove from the heat. Transfer the mixture to a food processor container and process into a puree. Refrigerate until ready for use.

To assemble the oysters for cooking, preheat the oven to 325 degrees. Spoon the cold sauce over the raw oysters in their half-shells. Sprinkle the grated Parmesan over the spinach mixture. Bake in the preheated oven for 20 minutes, or until the sauce is browned and bubbly. *Serves 6, allowing 6 oysters each.*

OYSTERS BIENVILLE

½ lb. ham, finely chopped
4 tbsp. butter (½ stick)
¾ cup diced yellow onion
⅓ cup diced sweet green bell
  pepper
⅓ cup diced red bell pepper
½ cup sliced fresh mushrooms
1 small garlic clove, minced
½ tsp. paprika
1 tsp. minced fresh basil leaves

½ tsp. cayenne pepper
½ cup flour
1 cup heavy cream
1 cup half & half
1 tsp. Worcestershire sauce
½ tsp. Tabasco sauce
Salt to taste
1½ lb. 70-90 count shrimp,
  peeled
36 oysters on the half-shell

Put the ham through a meat chopper with a large-hole disk. In a heavy saucepan melt the butter and sauté the onion, bell peppers, and mushrooms until the bell peppers are limp. Add the ham, garlic, paprika, basil, and cayenne. Sauté another 5 minutes, add the flour, and mix well. Sauté for 2 more minutes.

Add the heavy cream, half & half, Worcestershire, and Tabasco and mix well. Season to taste with salt. Add the shrimp and simmer until the mixture is very thick and will mound on a spoon. Adjust seasonings if desired. Refrigerate until ready for use.

To assemble the oysters for cooking, preheat the oven to 325 degrees. Spoon the cold sauce over the raw oysters in their half-shells. Bake in the preheated oven for 20 minutes, or until the sauce is browned and bubbly. *Serves 6, allowing 6 oysters each.*

OYSTERS LAFITTE

2 tbsp. fresh butter
2 tbsp. sliced green onions
1 tbsp. minced French shallots
1 tsp. minced garlic
½ cup white wine
Juice from 1 lemon
1¾ cups medium-thick Béchamel Sauce
1½ tbsp. fresh dill leaves, or 1½ tsp. dried

1½ lb. fresh boiled crawfish tail meat
Salt to taste
Pinch cayenne pepper
18 large raw oysters on the half-shell
¼ cup freshly grated Parmesan cheese
6 whole boiled crawfish for garnish

Preheat the oven to 350 degrees.

Melt the butter in a sauté or saucepan and sauté the green onions, French shallots, and garlic for 2 minutes without browning. Add the white wine, lemon juice, and reduce by half. Add the Béchamel Sauce, and dill and reduce by a third. Add the crawfish tails and simmer for 10 minutes. Salt to taste and add the cayenne pepper.

To assemble, spoon the crawfish mixture over raw oysters on the half-shell and place them on rock salt. Sprinkle with the freshly grated Parmesan cheese and bake in the preheated oven until the cheese is golden and the sauce is bubbling. Garnish each serving of three oysters with a boiled crawfish and serve. *Serves 6, allowing 3 oysters each.*

MUSSELS WITH TOMATOES AND CAPERS

36 mussels (about 2 qt.),
  scrubbed and bearded
1 cup dry white wine
2 tbsp. chopped shallots
½ tsp. dried thyme
1 bay leaf
¼ cup extra virgin olive oil
5 large Creole tomatoes, peeled,
  seeded, and cut into ¼-inch

to ½-inch dice
3 tbsp. chopped garlic
½ cup sliced green onions
¼ cup chopped fresh dill
1 tsp. white pepper
¼ cup "nonpareil" capers,
  rinsed
3 tbsp. chopped parsley

Cover and steam mussels in white wine with the shallots, thyme, and bay leaf for about 10 minutes. Remove mussels and cool, split shells leaving a mussel on each shell, and discard remaining half-shells. Reduce the mussel liquid by half and chill.

Combine the cold liquor with the olive oil, tomatoes, garlic, green onions, dill, and white pepper. Mix well. Top each mussel with some of the tomato mixture, then top each with several capers, sprinkle with the parsley, and serve. *Serves 6.*

SMOKED REDFISH

2 lb. rock salt
1 lb. dark brown sugar
1 small carrot, finely chopped
1 small leek, finely chopped
1 small onion, finely chopped
1 tsp. minced garlic
1 tbsp. black peppercorns,

freshly cracked
2 tbsp. fresh dill leaves
10 dried juniper berries,
  crushed, or 2 oz. (¼ cup) gin
1 1½-lb. redfish fillet (or fillets), scaled, unskinned
1¾ cups Fresh Dill Mayonnaise

Combine the rock salt and brown sugar with the carrot, leek, and onion. To this mixture add the garlic, peppercorns, dill, and juniper berries or gin.

In a container large enough to hold the mixture and the redfish fillet(s), spread half of the mixture evenly over the bottom. Now, lay the redfish fillets side by side, skin-side down, over the mixture bed and cover evenly with the remaining mixture. With a board or container slightly smaller than the original container, weigh down the fish in the mixture using just enough weight to keep fish from rising to the top. Refrigerate for 24 hours or until the fish flesh is "medium" to the touch.

Remove fillets from the mixture and rinse under cool running water. Pat dry with a clean towel and place in a conventional smoker and cold smoke for about three hours. To slice, place fish skin-side down and slice at a 30-degree angle into very thin 1½-inch-wide slices. Serve with Fresh Dill Mayonnaise. *Serves 6.*

TUNA OR SALMON CARPACCIO

1 lb. rock salt
¾ cup brown sugar
1 small carrot, finely chopped
½ cup chopped leek tops
¼ cup finely chopped celery
¼ cup finely chopped white onion
1 small clove garlic, pressed
¼ tsp. freshly ground black

pepper
½ cup chopped fresh dill, or 2 tbsp. dried dill
4 crushed dried juniper berries
1 lb. salmon or tuna fillet, unskinned
1½ cups Carpaccio Sauce
1¼ cups Gravlox Sauce

In an enamel, ceramic, or stainless container that will accommodate the fish fillet and curing ingredients, combine the rock salt, brown sugar, carrot, leek tops, celery, white onion, and garlic. Add the black pepper, dill, and crushed juniper berries and stir all of the ingredients together until well blended.

Cover the bottom of a stainless steel, ceramic, or enamel container or pan with half of this dry curing mixture. Lay the fish fillet into the pan and sprinkle the remaining half of the mixture over the top of the fillet.

Cover the fillet first with plastic wrap and then rest a plate or other container on top of the plastic, a container that covers the entire fillet. Weight this plate down with several cans of food, or a pot, or other object of some weight, and refrigerate for two days to dry-cure.

To serve, wipe the fish fillet with a clean dry cloth and slice paper thin with a very sharp knife. Lay several slices on a plate and serve with Carpaccio and Gravlox sauces. *Serves 6-8.*

CARPACCIO WITH BLACK PEPPERCORNS

1 lb. centercut beef tenderloin	¼ tsp. freshly ground black
½ cup fruity virgin olive oil	pepper
2 tbsp. freshly squeezed lemon	2 tbsp. green peppercorns,
juice	lightly bruised
1 tsp. salt	Toasted brown bread

Tightly wrap the meat in plastic wrap or foil and hold it in the freezer until it is quite stiff, yet not frozen. Now, with a very sharp knife, slice the meat across the grain into the thinnest slices that you can.

In an ceramic container, combine the olive oil with the lemon juice, salt, black pepper, and bruised green peppercorns. Lay the thinly sliced beef into this seasoning marinade/mixture, turning the slices so that they are completely coated with the marinade, cover, and refrigerate for three hours, or even better, overnight.

To serve the carpaccio, arrange the meat slices on chilled plates and garnish with lemon slices and brown bread. *Serves 6.*

CELERY ROOT TERRINE

3 lb. celery root or celeriac,
  peeled
2 qt. water
2 tbsp. all-purpose flour
1 tbsp. lemon juice
1¾ tsp. salt
3 medium French shallots,
  finely chopped
3½ cups (about 14 oz.) grated
  Gruyère cheese (reserve ¾

cup to coat loaf pan)
3 tbsp. heavy cream
2 eggs
½ tsp. finely ground white pepper
1 medium carrot, julienned
¼ cup green beans
¼ cup fresh baby peas
2 cups Raw Tomato-Basil Sauce

Preheat the oven to 350 degrees.

Cut the peeled celery root into 3-inch chunks.

Combine the water, flour, lemon juice, and ¼ tsp. of the salt in a saucepan. Bring the liquid to a boil and cook, while stirring, for 2 minutes. Add the celery root chunks and return the liquids to a simmer. Cover and cook for 15 minutes or until the celery root is tender. With a slotted spoon, transfer the celery root to a food processor container. Process into a puree and transfer the puree to a mixing bowl.

Add the shallots, Gruyère cheese, heavy cream, eggs, remaining salt, and white pepper. Adjust seasonings if desired. Hold aside.

Butter an 8-by-4-inch loaf pan. Sprinkle the reserved ¾ cup of grated Gruyère cheese into the mold, turning to coat both the bottom and sides of the mold.

Immerse carrot in a pan of boiling water and cook for 3 minutes or until soft. Drain and cool the carrot. Immerse the green beans in a pan of boiling water and cook for 6 minutes or until tender. Drain and cool. Immerse the fresh peas in a pan of boiling water and cook for 5 minutes or until tender.

Spoon a third of the celery puree into the mold and spread it out evenly. Place a row of green beans along the length of the pan. Repeat, alternating vegetables until puree is covered. Spoon another third of puree on top of the vegetables and add another layer of vegetables as above. Cover with the remaining puree.

Bake the terrine in the preheated oven for approximately 1 hour, or until the terrine is slightly puffed and a knife blade inserted into the center of the terrine comes out clean. Remove from oven and let cool.

Cover the terrine with plastic wrap and refrigerate overnight. To serve the terrine, unmold it and cut it into slices. Serve accompanied by Raw Tomato-Basil Sauce. *Makes 1 8-by-4-inch terrine.*

CHICKEN VEGETABLE TERRINE WITH BASIL PESTO MAYONNAISE

¾ cup cut broccoli
¾ cup cut cauliflower
¾ cup cut carrots
1 lb. chicken breast meat
1½ tsp. minced French shallots
1½ tsp. minced garlic

¾ tsp. minced fresh oregano leaves
½ cup egg whites
½ cup heavy cream
2 tsp. salt
½ tsp. white pepper
¾ cup Basil Pesto Mayonnaise

Preheat the oven to 350 degrees.

Cook vegetables separately in lightly salted water until they are tender, but not overcooked. Drain the vegetables, rinse under cool running water, and set aside to cool.

Divide the chicken meat into thirds. Transfer one third of the chicken to a food processor container and add the broccoli. Add ½ tsp. each of the shallots and garlic and ⅓ tsp. of the oregano. Process into a puree. Add a third of the egg whites and a third of the cream and season with a third of the salt and pepper. Process again until all is very smooth. Set aside. Repeat this process separately again for the cauliflower and the carrots.

Butter a 1½-quart loaf pan and line it with parchment paper. Transfer the broccoli mixture into the bottom of the pan and spread it out evenly. Now spread the cauliflower mixture evenly in the pan over the broccoli mixture and then the carrot mixture.

Place the loaf pan in a hot water bath and bake in the preheated oven for 45 minutes. Remove from the oven and cool slightly. Unmold the terrine onto a plate and allow it to cool thoroughly. Cover the terrine with plastic wrap and refrigerate overnight. Serve the terrine in slices on lettuce leaves with a dollop of the Pesto Mayonnaise. *Makes 1 quart loaf terrine.*

VEAL AND CHICKEN TERRINE

1½ lb. lean veal, cut into 1½-inch cubes
1½ lb. chicken white meat, skinless, cut into 1½-inch cubes
1½ lb. pork back fat, cut into 1½-inch cubes
1½ lb. morrels (mushrooms)
1 cup white wine
½ cup brandy
4 tbsp. Dijon mustard
2 tbsp. minced fresh basil
1½ tsp. minced French shallot

½ tsp. minced garlic
2 tsp. salt
½ tsp. black pepper
3 eggs
1 tbsp. cornstarch
Bacon for lining pan
6 slices pickled tongue (save half for garnish)
1 tbsp. green peppercorns (save half for garnish)
1 tbsp. chopped truffle (save half for garnish)

Preheat oven to 350 degrees.

In a covered container, combine the veal, chicken, and the pork back fat. Add the morrels, white wine, brandy, Dijon mustard, basil, shallot, garlic, salt, and pepper. Marinate overnight.

Process the meats and marinating mixture in a food processor until very fine. Continue processing the meats and add the eggs and cornstarch.

Line a 2-quart loaf pan with bacon and spoon in the prepared mixture. Garnish the top with half of the pickled tongue, green peppercorns, and truffle. Bake in a water bath in the preheated oven for two hours. Weigh down the terrine with a smaller container or board, cover, and refrigerate overnight. Serve in slices garnished with the remaining tongue, green peppercorns, and truffle. *Makes 1 quart loaf terrine.*

VEAL TERRINE

1½ lb. lean veal
1½ lb. pork Boston butt
1½ lb. Morel pork backfat
⅓ cup white wine
3 tbsp. brandy
3 tbsp. port wine
1½ tbsp. Dijon mustard
1½ tbsp. minced French shallot
1½ tsp. minced garlic
1½ tbsp. minced fresh basil, or basil and marjoram combined equally
2 tsp. salt
½ tsp. black pepper

½ lb. duck or rabbit livers
¼ cup brandy
¼ cup port wine
½ tsp. thyme leaves
3 eggs
1 tbsp. cornstarch
Bacon for lining pan
6 slices pickled tongue for garnish
1 tbsp. green peppercorns for garnish
1 tbsp. chopped truffle for garnish

Cut the veal, boston butt, and pork backfat into 1-inch cubes.

Combine the white wine, brandy, port wine, Dijon mustard, shallot, garlic, basil, salt, and pepper to make the marinade.

Place the cubed meats in a container and cover with the marinade mixture. Cover the container and refrigerate overnight.

In a separate container combine the livers with the brandy, port wine, and thyme. Cover and refrigerate overnight.

Preheat the oven to 350 degrees.

Process the meats and marinade in a food processor until medium fine. Drain the livers and add them to the mixture. Process for 30 seconds longer. Process in the eggs and cornstarch.

Line a 1½-quart loaf pan with bacon. Transfer the terrine mixture into the fat-lined loaf pan and garnish the top with pickled tongue, green peppercorns, and truffle. Bake in a hot water bath in the preheated oven for 2 hours. Weigh down the terrine with a smaller container and refrigerate overnight. Serve in slices. *Makes 1 quart loaf terrine.*

BOUDIN BLANC TERRINE
WITH RED ONION CONFIT

2 medium-sized yellow onions, chopped
1½ cups heavy cream
4 bay leaves
4 whole cloves
1 large garlic clove, minced
¼ tsp. dried thyme
Pinch ground nutmeg
1½ tbsp. salt
1 tsp. black pepper
8 French shallots, minced
1 tbsp. butter, plus some to
grease the loaf pan lining
1 lb. trimmed, lean pork loin, cut into 1-inch cubes
3 eggs
6 tbsp. all-purpose flour
¼ cup port wine
3 tbsp. dried currants, minced
Lettuce leaves
Cracked peppercorns
1½ cups Red Onion Confit
Toasted French bread rounds

In a saucepan, combine the yellow onions, heavy cream, bay leaves, cloves, garlic, thyme, nutmeg, salt, and black pepper. Add 1½ tablespoons of the minced shallots. Bring to simmer, remove from heat, cover, and let stand at room temperature for a half hour or so, until cool. Transfer the contents of the saucepan to a covered container and refrigerate overnight.

Preheat the oven to 325 degrees.

Line a 2-quart loaf pan or terrine with parchment paper or foil. Butter the inside of the lining. Melt the 1 tablespoon of butter in a sauté pan and sauté the remaining French shallots. Cook until soft.

In a food processor container, combine the cooked shallots, butter, pork cubes, eggs, flour, and port wine and process into a puree. With the food processor running, pour in the pork marinade slowly and allow it to be completely blended with the pork puree. Add the currants and stop processing.

Transfer the mixture into the prepared terrine or loaf pan. Place the pan in a larger pan and fill the larger pan with boiling water to an inch below the top edge of the terrine pan. Grease a piece of parchment or foil and cover the top of the terrine.

Place both pans to bake in the preheated oven for 1½ hours, or until the terrine begins to shrink from the sides of the pan and a small knife inserted into the center comes out clean. Uncover and allow to cool. When the terrine is room temperature, cover and refrigerate overnight.

To serve, line a dish or platter with lettuce leaves. Sit the terrine on the leaves and sprinkle the top with cracked peppercorns. Slice the terrine into individual servings and serve with Red Onion Confit and toasted French bread rounds. *Serves 6-8.*

DUCK RILLETS

1 6-lb. duckling	**4 fresh thyme sprigs**
⅓ bottle dry white wine	**Salt and black pepper**
1 onion, sliced	**1 cup clarified butter**
1 clove garlic, peeled and chopped	**French bread**

Preheat the oven to 400 degrees. Quarter the duckling and brown in the preheated oven until fat begins to render, about 30 minutes. Turn the pieces to achieve an even brownness. Add the white wine, onion, garlic, and thyme and cook until duck is done. Set aside to cool.

Strain the juice and fat from the pan. Shred the duck meat and skin and discard the bones. Add the skin and meat to the strained fat and juices. Mix with a wooden spoon and season with the salt and black pepper. Use plenty of black pepper.

When chilled or until stiff, stirring every 15 minutes, spoon the rillets into small crocks and top to seal with the clarified butter. Refrigerate. Serve cold with French bread. *Makes 2½ lb.*

ESCARGOT BOURGUIGNONNE

3 cups Brown Sauce #2
1 cup red wine
1 tbsp. chopped green onion
½ tbsp. chopped French shallots
1 tsp. chopped garlic

3 tbsp. butter
Salt to taste
Black Pepper to taste
3 dozen "escargot" snails

In a saucepan, combine the Brown Sauce with the red wine, green onions, shallots, garlic, and butter. Bring to a boil and reduce to a simmer. Season to taste with salt and black pepper.

Add the snails to the sauce in the pan and simmer for about 8 minutes. Adjust seasoning, if desired, and remove from the heat.

Serve the snails six to the serving in a snail dish, in their shells, or in a small ramekin with the sauce. *Serves 6, allowing 6 escargot each.*

DAUBE GLACE
WITH CREOLE MUSTARD DRESSING

¼ cup corn oil
2 lb. beef chuck roast
1 pig's foot, split
Salt
2 medium carrots, peeled and
   diced
1 cup sliced leeks
½ cup chopped green onions
½ tsp. minced garlic
1 tsp. minced parsley
2 bay leaves

¼ tsp. ground thyme leaves
¼ tsp. freshly ground black
   pepper
1/16 tsp. ground cloves
1/16 tsp. cayenne pepper
¼ cup red wine
1 tbsp. red wine vinegar
Water to cover
1 1/3 cups Creole Mustard Dressing (Horseradish Creole
   Mustard Cream)

In a heavy Dutch oven or covered soup pot, heat the corn oil. Sprinkle the beef chuck roast liberally with salt and carefully lay it in the heated oil. Cook the roast, turning from time to time, until all sides are nicely browned, approximately 10 minutes.

Add the split pig's foot, the carrots, leeks, green onions, garlic, and parsley. Continue cooking, stirring from time to time to prevent any sticking. Add the bay leaves, thyme, black pepper, cloves, and cayenne pepper. Continue cooking until the onions begin to color.

Deglaze the pot with the red wine and red wine vinegar and scrape the bottom to loosen any browned juices. Now, add enough water to the pot to just cover all of the ingredients. Cover the pot and bring the liquids to a gentle simmer. Simmer for 3-3½ hours, or until the roast and pig's foot are very tender.

Carefully lift the pig's foot from the pot and lay it on a plate. Remove and discard the bones. Chop the remaining meat and return it to the pot.

Transfer the roast from the pot to a plate or chopping board. Cut the meat into large dice or cubes. Return the cubed roast to the pot and stir all well together. Remove the pot from the heat and, using a ladle, transfer its contents into a loaf pan.

Lay a sheet of plastic wrap into the loaf pan to cover its contents and refrigerate overnight, or until gelled.

To serve, unmold the Daube Glace from its pan. To do this, remove the plastic wrap. Fill another pan large enough to accommodate the loaf pan with hot water and hold the loaf pan in the water as deep as its contents. Do not let any hot water run into the loaf pan. Hold for about 5-10 seconds and remove the loaf pan from the water. Place a plate or platter over the top of the loaf mold and flip the whole thing over. The Daube Glace will slip out of the mold and onto the plate. Slice the loaf into six or eight pieces and serve on chilled salad plates accompanied with Creole Mustard Dressing. *Serves 6-8*.

Soups

"WHITE" GAZPACHO

3 medium-sized cucumbers,
  skinned, seeded, and diced
1 large rib celery, diced
1 small sweet green bell pepper,
  diced
2 green onions, chopped
1 small clove garlic, pressed
½ cup water
2 tbsp. white vinegar
3-inch piece French bread,
  shredded
1 qt. plain yogurt
Salt to taste
White pepper to taste
Dash cayenne pepper
½ sweet red bell pepper, diced
  small
½ sweet green bell pepper,
  diced small
1 small cucumber, diced small

In the container of a food processor or blender, combine the cucumber, celery, green bell pepper, green onions, garlic, water, white vinegar, and shredded French bread. Process until very smooth.

Add the yogurt and season to taste with salt, white pepper, and cayenne pepper. Pass the mixture through a china cap, tamis, or strainer.

To serve the soup, fold in the diced red bell pepper, green bell pepper, and cucumber. Stir until diced vegetables are evenly distributed throughout the soup. *Makes approximately 1¾ quarts.*

RED GAZPACHO

2 cucumbers, skinned, seeded,
  and diced small
1 small sweet green bell pepper, seeded and diced small
1 small sweet red pepper,
  seeded and diced small
½ small yellow onion, chopped
  fine
1 small rib celery, chopped fine
1 tsp. minced garlic
4½ cups tomato juice
1 10-oz. can beef broth
2 tbsp. Worcestershire sauce
½ tsp. Tabasco sauce
1 tsp. ground cumin
Salt to taste
Black pepper to taste

In a container, combine the cucumbers, green bell pepper, red bell pepper, yellow onion, celery, and garlic. Stir in the tomato juice, beef broth, Worcestershire sauce, Tabasco sauce, and ground cumin. Season to taste with salt and black pepper. Cover the container and refrigerate overnight, or until cold. *Makes 2 quarts.*

Note: You can substitute a prepared Bloody Mary mix for the plain tomato juice, but omit the Worcestershire sauce and Tabasco sauce.

COLD APPLE SOUP

4 apples, cored, skinned, and
   sliced
1½ cups apple juice
1½ tbsp. lemon juice
1½ tsp. sugar

1 small cinnamon stick
1½ cups half & half
1 cup orange juice
⅓ tsp. vanilla

In a saucepan, combine the sliced apples, apple juice, lemon juice, sugar, and cinnamon stick. Bring to a simmer, cover, and cook for 20 minutes, or until the sliced apples are very soft and break apart at a touch. Remove from the heat and cool.

Remove and discard the cinnamon stick, add the half & half, the orange juice, and vanilla. Transfer the soup to a blender and process until smooth. Store the soup in a covered container in the refrigerator until cold and then serve. *Serves 6.*

CLEAR ARTICHOKE SOUP

1 small yellow onion, diced
1 tbsp. olive oil
1 clove garlic, minced
1 14-oz. can artichoke hearts,
   partially crushed, packing
   liquids reserved

1 qt. plus 1 cup chicken stock
1 tbsp. white vinegar
Salt to taste
White pepper to taste
Pinch cayenne pepper

In a saucepan or soup pot, sauté the yellow onions in the olive oil over medium heat until clear: *do not brown*. Add the garlic and artichoke hearts and stir until heated. Add the chicken stock, reserved artichoke packing liquids, and white vinegar. Season to taste with salt, if necessary, white pepper, and cayenne pepper. Bring to a boil, remove from heat, and serve. *Serves 6.*

CLEAR LEEK SOUP
WITH APPLE-SMOKED BACON

¼ lb. sliced apple-smoked
   bacon
½ lb. sliced leeks, white part
   only

1 tbsp. chopped garlic
1 qt. chicken stock
Salt to taste
White pepper to taste

Brown the bacon in a soup pot and add the leeks and garlic. Sauté for about 5 minutes. Add the chicken stock, bring to a boil, and simmer for 10 minutes. Season to taste with salt and white pepper and serve. *Serves 6.*

CREAM OF LEEK CHANTILLY

3-4 medium-sized leeks, white
   part only, well washed and
   finely sliced
1 tbsp. minced garlic
4 tbsp. fresh butter
5 tbsp. all-purpose flour
5 cups stock from leek trimmings

2 chicken bouillon cubes
2 bay leaves
½ cup heavy cream
Salt to taste
White pepper to taste
1 cup freshly whipped heavy
   cream

Sauté the leeks and garlic gently in butter until they begin to turn clear. Add the flour while stirring constantly, and cook for 10 minutes without browning to make the roux.

Add the leek stock in three stages, mixing thoroughly each time. Add the chicken bouillon cubes and bay leaves and simmer gently for about 30 minutes. Finally, add the heavy cream, season to taste with salt and white pepper, and simmer 10 minutes more.

To serve, ladle the boiling soup into hot cups or bowls and garnish each serving with a dollop of freshly whipped cream. *Serves 6.*

CREAM OF TOMATO SOUP

4 tbsp. butter
2 medium carrots, chopped
2 medium onions, chopped
¾ cup flour—the wheat, barley,
   or rice variety
1½ qt. hot chicken stock
1 qt. canned Italian tomato
   puree
1 leek, chopped

2 stalks celery, chopped
6 large tomatoes, chopped
1 clove garlic, chopped
8 white peppercorns
1 tbsp. sugar
½ tbsp. salt
1 cup heavy cream
1 tbsp. butter

In a soup kettle, melt 4 tbsp. butter. Add the carrots and onions and sauté them until they turn golden. Blend in the flour and cook the mixture for a few minutes.

Gradually whisk in the hot chicken stock and simmer, stirring constantly, until it is thick and smooth. Water may be used instead of stock, but add some chicken bones or a small bird, cleaned and trussed, and, if available, a veal knuckle parboiled in salted water and drained.

Add the tomato puree, leeks, celery, tomatoes, garlic, peppercorns, sugar, and salt. Simmer the soup for 2 hours, skimming if necessary. Remove the bones or fowl and force the soup through a fine sieve.

Just before serving, bring the soup back to a boil and add the cream and 1 tbsp. butter. If the soup is too thick, add a little milk. Season with salt if necessary and serve. *Serves 12.*

CREAM OF CARROT SOUP

2 tbsp. butter
4 medium carrots, thinly sliced
1 onion, diced
1 qt. chicken stock
½ cup rice

1 tbsp. sugar
1 tsp. salt
2 cups hot water
1 cup light cream
1 tbsp. butter

In a soup kettle, melt the butter and add the carrots and onions. Cover the kettle and sauté the vegetables slowly for 15 minutes without letting them brown. Add the chicken stock, rice, sugar, and salt. Simmer the soup for 45 minutes, or until the rice is very soft. Then force the mixture through a fine sieve or food mill, return it to the kettle, and add the hot water. Bring the soup back to a boil and add the light cream and butter. Season with salt. *Serves 6.*

CREAM OF FRESH CELERY SOUP

¼ lb. butter
1 cup celery, chopped with
   leaves
1 small onion, chopped
1 tbsp. garlic, chopped
½ cup all-purpose flour
2 cups beef broth

1 cup water
Salt to taste
Black pepper to taste
1 cup heavy cream
Chopped parsley for garnish
Grated nutmeg for garnish

Melt the butter in a soup pot. Add the celery, onions, and garlic to cook for 5 minutes, being careful they do not brown. Add the flour and cook 10 minutes more. Whisk in the beef broth and water and blend well. Simmer for 15 minutes. Season to taste with salt and pepper. Add the heavy cream and return to a boil. Simmer for 10 minutes more. Garnish each serving with fresh, chopped parsley and a fresh grating of nutmeg. *Serves 4.*

LENTIL SOUP

½ lb. bacon, diced
2 medium-sized potatoes,
 peeled and diced
1 small carrot, diced
1 rib celery, diced
1 small onion, diced
¾ lb. smoked pork sausage,
 sliced

1 lb. dried lentils, washed
5 cups chicken broth
Salt to taste
White pepper to taste
1 tbsp. red wine vinegar, or to
 taste

In a saucepan or soup pot, cook the diced bacon until it is almost browned. Add the potatoes, carrots, celery, and onions. Cook until the vegetables begin to soften, and then add the sausage. Cook together for another 5 minutes. Add the dried lentils and chicken broth and simmer for 45 minutes to 1 hour, or until the lentils are cooked. Adjust seasoning if desired, add red wine vinegar, and serve. *Serves 6.*

SHRIMP BISQUE

2 tbsp. butter
½ carrot, finely chopped
½ onion, finely chopped
2 sprigs parsley
½ bay leaf
Pinch thyme
1 cup white wine
24 whole raw medium shrimp,
 washed

¾ cup flour
2 qt. chicken stock
3 tbsp. cream
2 tbsp. butter
2 tbsp. brandy, sherry, or
 Madeira

In a large saucepan, melt 2 tbsp. butter and add the carrots, onions, parsley, bay leaf, and thyme. Cover the pan and cook the vegetables slowly until they are tender. Add the white wine and the shrimp and poach them for about 8 minutes. Remove and reserve the shrimp.

When the shrimp are cool enough to handle, shell and devein twelve of them, reserving the shells. Cut the meat into dice and reserve it. Put the shells and the remaining whole shrimp through the food chopper and add the chopped mixture to the kettle with the mirepoix and poaching wine. Stir in the flour. Add the chicken stock, bring the soup to a boil, and simmer it for 20 minutes. Strain it through a fine sieve and, if it is too thick, add a little milk. Strain it again through a thickness of cheesecloth.

Just before serving, bring the soup back to a boil and add the cream and 2 tbsp. each of butter and brandy, sherry, or Madeira. Garnish each serving with the reserved diced shrimp. *Serves 12.*

SHRIMP BISQUE CORDON BLEU

2 tbsp. butter
40 small raw shrimp (50 count),
  peeled and deveined
2 tbsp. flour
¾ tsp. paprika
Pinch cayenne pepper
4 cups double-strength hot
  shrimp stock

2 tbsp. brandy
1½ cups half & half, heated
1 minced dry shallot
1 clove garlic, minced
Salt to taste
White pepper to taste
½ cup freshly whipped cream

Melt the butter in a sauté pan, sauté the shrimp, and add the flour. Stir and cook as for a roux, but do not brown. Add the paprika and cayenne, then add the hot shrimp stock and brandy; whisk thoroughly. Bring to a simmer and add the half & half, shallots, and garlic. Season to taste with salt and white pepper. Simmer for 10 minutes.

For each serving, add the desired number and size of cooked shrimp, top soup with freshly whipped cream and serve. *Serves 6.*

MIRLITON AND SHRIMP SOUP

3 medium-sized mirlitons
4 cups seafood stock or water
½ cup butter
4 tbsp. flour
¾ cup diced celery
⅓ cup diced carrots
¼ cup diced onions
⅓ cup sliced leeks

1 tbsp. garlic
2 bay leaves
1 cup peeled and deveined
  shrimp
2 cups heated heavy cream
¾ cup sauterne wine
1½ tsp. salt
½ tsp. white pepper

Pare and dice mirlitons and melt butter in suitable soup pot. Add flour, blend, and cook for 2 minutes. Add celery, carrots, onions, leeks, garlic, and bay leaves and cook for 5 minutes.

Add the shrimp and mirlitons, mix thoroughly, and allow to heat through. Strain stock into soup pot stirring all the while, then add the hot cream and sauterne. Simmer about 30 minutes and stir occasionally. Add salt and pepper. Serve. *Makes 1½ quarts, which serves 6.*

SHRIMP AND CURRY BISQUE

2 tbsp. olive oil
¾ cup diced celery
¾ cup diced carrots
½ cup diced yellow onion
1 lb. 26-30 count shrimp,
  peeled, deveined, and
  chopped
2 tbsp. tomato paste
¼ cup brandy
¼ qt. shellfish or fish stock, or
  clam juice

2 tbsp. butter
1 tbsp. curry powder
½ tbsp. ground nutmeg
¼ tsp. ground cinnamon
¼ cup flour
½ qt. heavy cream or half & half
Salt to taste
Black pepper to taste
Louisiana hot sauce to taste
6 lemon slices for garnish
Fresh dill

Heat the olive oil in a soup pot. Add the diced celery, carrots, yellow onion, and shrimp. Sauté together until the shrimp are opaque, about 5 minutes. Add the tomato paste and brandy and simmer 5 minutes. Then add the shellfish or fish stock, or clam juice, bring to a boil, reduce heat, and simmer for 1 hour. Strain mixture.

In another large saucepan or soup pot, melt the butter; add the curry powder, nutmeg, and cinnamon; and blend in the flour. Cook while stirring until the mixture foams up and the raw flour aroma becomes a cooking bread aroma. Whisk this mixture, the roux, a little at a time, into the soup and simmer for 20 minutes, stirring occasionally.

Whisk the heavy cream or half & half into the bisque and simmer for 5 minutes. Season to taste with salt, white pepper, and Louisiana hot sauce. To serve, garnish each portion with a lemon slice and fresh dill. *Serves 6.*

CRAWFISH BISQUE

2 tbsp. butter	1 cup white wine
½ carrot, finely chopped	½ cup fish stock or water
½ onion, finely chopped	½ tsp. salt
2 sprigs parsley, chopped	Black pepper to taste
1 small bay leaf	¾ cup flour
Pinch dried thyme	2 qt. chicken stock
30 crawfish, peeled and deveined	3 tbsp. cream
	2 tbsp. butter
2 tbsp. brandy, hot	2 tbsp. brandy

Make a mirepoix—a cooked vegetable seasoning base—as follows: In a large saucepan, melt the butter and add the carrot, onion, parsley, bay leaf, and thyme. Cover the pan and cook the vegetables until they are tender, about 6 minutes.

Lay the crawfish tail meat on the mirepoix and cook them, covered, until they are bright red. Add the hot brandy and ignite. When the flame burns out, add the white wine, fish stock or water, salt, and pepper. Cover the pan and poach the crawfish for 10-12 minutes. Remove the meat from the bodies and tails, remove and discard the intestinal vein.

Put the shells through the food chopper and return them to the kettle with the mirepoix and poaching liquid. Stir in the flour. Add the chicken stock and bring the soup to a boil for a few minutes. When the sauce is thickened, strain it through a fine sieve. If it seems too thick, add a little milk. Strain it again through a double thickness of cheesecloth.

Just before serving, bring the soup back to a boil and add the cream, butter, and brandy. Cut the reserved crawfish tail meat into small pieces and add them to the pot. Boil for 1 minute more and serve. *Serves 12.*

LOBSTER BISQUE

1 live 1½- to 2-lb. lobster	1 cup cream
¼ cup brandy	Salt to taste
2 qt. chicken stock	2 tbsp. sherry
¾ cup flour	

Split a live lobster down the back and remove the intestinal vein and the sac of gritty matter in the head. Using a heavy butcher's knife, cut the lobster crosswise into several pieces. Put the pieces in a soup kettle with the brandy and chicken stock. Bring the liquid to a boil and simmer the lobster for 20-25 minutes.

Remove the meat from the lobster shells and reserve it. Put the more tender shells through a food chopper and return them to the soup kettle. Stir in the flour. If the soup seems too thick, add a little water. Simmer for 25 minutes, then strain through a fine sieve.

Add the cream and season with salt. Strain the soup again through a double thickness of cheesecloth. Just before serving, bring the soup back to a boil and add the sherry and a few small dice of lobster meat. Use the remaining lobster meat for salads or other dishes. *Serves 12.*

ESCARGOT HERBSAINT BISQUE

½ cup oil or butter
½ cup diced carrots
¼ cup diced celery
¼ cup diced onions
1 tbsp. chopped garlic
1 cup escargots, halved length-
    wise, packing liquid reserved
½ cup flour
2½ cups hot veal or chicken
    stock (with escargot juice)

1½ cups heated heavy cream,
    heated
Salt to taste
White pepper to taste
⅓ cup Herbsaint or Pernod (or
    to taste)
1 tbsp. fresh chopped parsley
1 cup freshly whipped heavy
    cream

In large saucepan or soup pot, in the oil or butter, sauté the diced carrots, celery, and onions until they are soft. Add the garlic and escargots and continue to sauté for 5 more minutes. Then blend in the flour and cook for 3-4 minutes. Whisk in the hot veal or chicken stock with any escargot juice that you may have from the can. Add the heated heavy cream and bring to a boil, stirring occasionally, and turn down to a simmer.

Season to taste with the salt and white pepper and add the Herbsaint or Pernod. Bring to a boil again and add the parsley. Ladle the soup into bowls and garnish each serving with a dollop of freshly whipped cream. *Serves 6.*

BOUILLABAISSE

BROTH

½ lb. carrots, chopped
½ lb. celery ribs, chopped
½ lb. onions, chopped
½ lb. fennel
½ lb. green peppers, chopped
½ cup olive oil
1 tbsp. cup chopped garlic
¼ cup chopped shallots

½ cup tomato paste
1 gallon shrimp or fish stock
2 cups chopped tomatoes
⅛ oz. saffron
Salt to taste
White pepper to taste
3 bay leaves

Peel and split the carrots and slice them diagonally; slice the celery the same way. Also cut the onions, fennel, and green peppers in a similar fashion.

In a suitable stock pot heat the olive oil, sauté the carrots, celery, and fennel until half-cooked. Add the onions, peppers, garlic, and shallots.

When the mixture is thoroughly heated, stir in the tomato paste and cook for 10 minutes, stirring regularly. Then add the stock, preferably lukewarm. Add the tomatoes, crushing and draining by hand as you go. Then add the saffron, already "steeped" in hot water, salt and pepper, and bay leaves. Bring to a full boil, remove from heat, cool, and chill.

BOUILLABAISSE SEAFOOD INGREDIENTS

1 lb. peeled, deveined, raw
   shrimp
1 cup raw oysters
½ lb. lump crabmeat
½ lb. peeled crawfish tail meat

½ lb. fresh fish, trout, pompano, etc., cut into 1-inch
   cubes
½ lb. raw scallops
18 fresh mussels

When ready to complete and serve the Bouillabaisse, heat the broth in a soup pot to a boil. Add the shrimp, oysters, crabmeat, crawfish, fish, scallops, and mussels. Bring back to a simmer and cook for only about 5 minutes, or just enough time for the seafood to be cooked but not overdone. Serve. *Serves 6.*

CREAM OF GAMEBIRD SOUP

2 tbsp. butter
Bones from a roasted pheasant,
    partridge, guinea hen, or
    other fowl
¾ cup wheat flour
6 tbsp. dry sherry or Madeira

1½ qt. chicken stock
1 cup heavy cream
Salt to taste
½ cup cooked gamebird meat,
    julienned or diced

In a soup kettle, melt the butter and add the bones of the bird. Cook them until they take on a rich brown color. Add the wheat flour, sherry or Madeira, and the chicken stock. Simmer the soup for 1½ hours. Remove the bones. Add the cream and season with salt. Strain the soup through a fine sieve and add the cooked gamebird meat.

Heat for 1 minute more and serve. *Serves 12.*

TURTLE SOUP

STOCK

2 lb. turtle meat
1 gallon water
½ tsp. thyme
2 ribs celery with leaves,
    chopped coarsely
3 onions, quartered

2 carrots, chopped coarsely
6 sprigs parsley
6 cloves
6 whole allspice
6 black peppercorns
1 garlic clove

Remove and discard all skin and fat from the turtle meat. Put the meat in the cold water, heating slowly, and skim off any scum that rises. When well skimmed, add all of the remaining ingredients and cook until tender, about 2 hours.

Remove the meat and strain stock. If necessary, add beef or chicken bouillon to make three quarts of liquid. Debone the turtle meat and process the meat in a food mill, using a steel blade. This may be done the day before. Store stock and meat separately in the refrigerator.

SOUP

½ cup butter or cooking oil, or half butter and half oil

½ cup all-purpose flour

½ cup green onions, finely minced

2 medium onions, finely chopped

2 8-oz. cans tomato sauce

⅓ cup lean ham, ground or minced

1 bunch flat leaf parsley, minced

1 bay leaf

½ tsp. dried thyme leaves, crushed (rub between hands)

2 cloves garlic, minced

3 tbsp. lemon juice

½ tsp. black pepper, freshly ground

¼ tsp. Louisiana hot sauce or to taste

Salt to taste

4 hard-boiled eggs, minced

2 cups Amontillado sherry

1 lemon, thinly sliced and seeded

In a soup pot, heat the butter and or oil, but do not let it brown. Add the flour and make a medium-brown roux. Add the green onions and onions and cook until soft. Add the tomato sauce and cook for 5 minutes. Add the ham, cooked turtle meat, and parsley and cook for 5 minutes. Add all of the remaining ingredients, except the sliced lemon and mix well.

Reheat the stock and add it gradually, stirring well, and boil gently for 2 hours. Additional ground allspice may be added if desired. Garnish each serving with a thin slice of lemon. Additional sherry may be added to taste. *Serves 8.*

Salads and Vegetables

SPRING SALAD

½ tsp. salt
½ tsp. dry mustard
Pinch pepper
2 tbsp. red-wine vinegar
6 tbsp. olive oil
½ cup cooked asparagus stalks, cut in pieces
½ cup cooked peas

½ cup radishes, sliced
2 artichoke bottoms, cooked and sliced
2 hard-boiled eggs, chopped
1 tsp. "fines herbes" (can be purchased from a store)
¼ cup mayonnaise

In a salad bowl, combine the salt, mustard, pepper, red-wine vinegar, and olive oil. Whisk well together, then add the asparagus pieces, peas, radishes, artichoke bottoms, eggs, and fines herbes. Toss gently, cover, and marinate for ½-1 hour in the refrigerator. Just before serving, carefully fold in the mayonnaise so as not to crush the vegetables. *Serves 6.*

SALAD BROUSSARD

12 endive leaves
1½ cups chopped iceberg lettuce
1½ cups chopped bibb lettuce
1½ cups chopped radiccio

3 medium tomatoes, cut into 6 slices each
1½ dozen pickled string beans
1½ dozen pickled okra

Place the two endive leaves on each of six chilled salad plates. Top with chopped iceberg and bibb lettuce and radiccio. Arrange three slices of tomatoes on each salad and garnish with three pickled string beans and three pickled okra. Serve with your choice of dressing. *Serves 6.*

MARINATED CELERIAC SALAD

Enough salted water to cover
2 to 3 whole celeriac (celery root)
¾ cup olive oil
¼ cup white vinegar
½ cup sliced green onions
½ medium white onion, sliced
Salt
White pepper

In a large pot boil the whole celery roots in lightly salted water for about 20 minutes, or until just fork-tender all the way through. Remove from water and cool completely. Peel each root well, removing any traces of brown skin or "eyes." Cut each root in half and then cut into in ¼-inch slices. Lay slices in a container in a shingled fashion.

Combine the olive oil, vinegar, green, and white onions and season to taste with salt and white pepper. Pour this marinade over the celery root. Move and loosen slices to allow marinade to penetrate each slice. Marinate at least 24 hours before serving. Remove from marinade and drain.

Serve the celery root with whatever lettuce or other greens that you prefer. *Serves 6.*

AVOCADO PASADENA

2½ cups crabmeat
2 tomatoes, peeled, seeded, and
    chopped
1 tbsp. tarragon vinegar
1 tsp. chopped chives
1 tbsp. mixed chopped parsley,
    tarragon, and chervil
1½ cups mayonnaise
2 tbsp. chili sauce
1 tbsp. Worcestershire sauce
Salt and white pepper
3 avocados, peeled, halved, and
    pits removed
3 ripe olives, pitted and halved

In a salad bowl, combine the crabmeat and tomatoes, then fold in the vinegar, chives, parsley, tarragon, and chervil. Into this combination fold the mayonnaise, chili sauce, and Worcestershire sauce. When all of this is well combined, season with salt and white pepper. Spoon the crabmeat mixture into the avocado halves and garnish each with half of a ripe olive. *Serves 6.*

FRESH AVOCADO, TOMATO, ASPARAGUS SALAD

1½ dozen trimmed fresh
  asparagus spears
Enough salted water to cover
  asparagus
1½ cups chopped iceberg lettuce
1½ cups chopped bibb lettuce
1½ cups chopped radiccio
3 small avocadoes
3 medium tomatoes, cut into 6
  slices each

Cook the asparagus in salted water. Do not overcook them. Allow to chill in the refrigerator in a little of their cooking water. Combine the iceberg, bibb, and radiccio lettuces and divide the mixture onto six chilled salad plates. Drain the chilled asparagus and arrange them on the lettuce beds.

Halve and skin the avocadoes. Cut them into slices. Arrange the avocado slices between the asparagus spears and garnish with the tomato slices. Serve the salad with your choice of dressing. *Serves 6.*

ASPARAGUS SALAD

36 asparagus stalks
Enough salted water to cover
  asparagus
2 eggs, hard-boiled and chilled
1 tbsp. chopped parsley
Lettuce
2 cups Creole Vinaigrette
  Dressing

Snap the tough ends from the asparagus stalks. Wash them well, flushing water through the tips to dislodge all sand. Cook the asparagus in boiling salted water until tender, then plunge into cold water to chill quickly, and drain on a towel.

Chop the chilled eggs and add the parsley. Arrange the asparagus on lettuce on individual plates and sprinkle it with the egg and parsley mixture. Serve with Creole Vinaigrette Dressing spooned over each salad. *Serves 6.*

HEARTS OF PALM
AND FRESH ASPARAGUS SALAD

1½ dozen trimmed fresh
    asparagus spears
Enough salted water to cover
    asparagus
1½ cups chopped iceberg lettuce
1½ cups chopped bibb lettuce

1½ cups chopped radiccio
3 medium tomatoes, cut into 6
    slices each
1 can hearts of palm, drained
    and halved lengthwise

Cook the asparagus in salted water. Do not overcook them. Allow to chill in the refrigerator in a little of their cooking water. Combine the iceberg, bibb, and radiccio lettuces and divide the mixture onto six chilled salad plates. Arrange three tomato slices on each bed of lettuce.

Drain the chilled asparagus and arrange them on the lettuce beds with the halved hearts of palm. Serve the salad with your choice of dressing. *Serves 6.*

TOMATO RING

5 cups tomato juice
3-4 very ripe fresh tomatoes, cut
    into pieces
½ tsp. sugar
1 clove
½ bay leaf

½ tsp. salt
2 tbsp. gelatin
½ cup cold water
Juice from 1 lemon
Your choice of vegetable salad

Combine tomato juice, tomatoes, sugar, clove, bay leaf, and salt and simmer the mixture for 10 minutes. Soften the gelatin in the cold water and stir it into the pot. Remove from the heat and add the lemon juice. Strain the mixture through a fine sieve.

Fill a ring mold and chill the jelly in the refrigerator until it is set. Unmold the ring on a serving dish and fill the center with a vegetable salad. *Serves 8.*

POTATO SALAD

6 medium potatoes, unpeeled
Enough salted water to cover
    potatoes
1 tsp. salt
Pepper to taste
2-3 tbsp. vinegar
6-7 tbsp. olive oil

¼ cup stock or hot water
1 tbsp. chopped parsley
1 tbsp. chopped chives
1 tbsp. chopped chervil
1 tbsp. chopped fresh tarragon
3 green onions, chopped

Boil the potatoes, unpeeled, in the salted water until they are tender. Drain, peel, and cut them into thin slices. While the potatoes are still hot, season them with the salt and pepper. Sprinkle with the vinegar and add olive oil. Add the stock and the parsley, chives, chervil, tarragon, and green onions.

Let the salad stand at room temperature until most of the liquid is absorbed. Serve the salad without chilling. *Serves 6.*

EGG NEST SALAD

4 cups shredded lettuce
12 hard-boiled eggs, sliced or
    quartered
1 cup mayonnaise
¼ cup heavy cream

2 tsp. Worcestershire sauce, or
    to taste
Salt to taste
Paprika for garnish

Arrange the shredded lettuce in the shape of birds' nests in equal portions on six chilled salad plates. Place the eggs in the center of the nests. Blend the mayonnaise thoroughly with the cream, Worcestershire sauce, and salt. Spoon the dressing over the eggs and nests and sprinkle with paprika. *Serves 6.*

BEET SALAD

6 medium beets, washed
2 cups Creole Vinaigrette
   Dressing

½ cup chopped green onions
6 lettuce leaves

Preheat the oven to 375 degrees.

Wash the beets and bake them in the preheated oven for about 40 minutes, or until tender. Cool, peel, and cut the beets into julienne pieces. Combine the beets with the green onions and dressing. Mix very carefully to avoid breaking the beets. Lay a lettuce leaf on each of six salad plates. Spoon the dressed beets onto the leaves. *Serves 6.*

FISH SALAD

1 lb. cooked fish fillet: salmon,
   halibut, tuna, or striped bass.
1 cup cooked lima beans
1 cup cooked peas
1 cup cooked diced carrots
1 cup mayonnaise
Salt and white pepper

Hot sauce to taste (optional)
Lettuce leaves to line salad
   bowl
2 tomatoes, quartered
1 cucumber, cut in six strips
2 hard-boiled eggs, quartered
2 lemons, quartered

Cut the fish into bite-sized pieces and fold together with the lima beans, peas, and diced carrots. Fold in the mayonnaise. Season with the salt, white pepper, and hot sauce, if desired. Line a salad bowl with the lettuce leaves and spoon the salad into the bowl.

Arrange in a decorative, alternating manner around the top of the salad, the tomatoes, cucumber, and eggs. Serve with lemon wedges. *Serves 6.*

SAUTEED CELERY

3 cups julienned celery
2 tbsp. butter
1 tsp. chopped dry shallots
Salt to taste

White pepper to taste
1 tbsp. chopped parsley

In a heated skillet, sauté the celery in the butter until it is half-cooked. Add the chopped shallots, season to taste with the salt and white pepper, and finish cooking. Add the parsley last, toss, and keep warm. *Serves 6.*

This vegetable goes well with all sauteed fish, game, and veal dishes.

Note: Julienned celery root—celeriac—is a terrific substitution here.

SAUTEED APPLES

3 large, firm-textured apples, skinned, cored, and cut into ½-inch wedges
4 tbsp. butter

Salt to taste
White pepper to taste
1½ tbsp. apple cider vinegar

In a heated skillet, melt the butter and sauté the apple wedges. Sauté until just done. Season to taste with salt and white pepper. Add the vinegar and toss well. Hold aside warm. *Serves 6.*

Serve these with duck, veal, game, and pork.

Note: It is advisable to cut apples at the last moment before cooking to prevent them from oxidizing (turning brown). But you may cut them beforehand and soak in water containing a little lemon juice, which will retard browning.

APPLE SHALLOT MINCEMEAT

3 qt. coarsely chopped, peeled, cored apples
½ cup diced dry shallots
Zest of 2 oranges
Zest of 1 lemon
¼ cup cider vinegar

2½ cups packed light brown sugar
1 tsp. ground cinnamon
¼ tsp. ground allspice
¼ tsp. ground cloves
¼ tsp. ground dried ginger

In a heavy pot, combine the chopped apples, shallot, zest of orange and lemon and cider vinegar. Stir in the light brown sugar and add the cinnamon, allspice, clove and ginger. Bring the mixture to a boil and turn down to a simmer. Simmer for about one hour, or until the apples are soft. Cool. Transfer to a covered container and store in the refrigerator for 1 week before using. *Makes about 1 ½ quarts.*

This is a good side dish for pork and game.

CREAMED SPINACH

2 tbsp. butter
2 tbsp. flour
1 lb. chopped spinach, fresh or defrosted
½ cup minced white onion

1 tsp. finely chopped garlic
1 tsp. finely chopped shallots
½ cup heavy cream
Salt to taste
Black pepper to taste

Melt butter in a saucepan and blend in the flour. Cook this mixture, the roux, slowly for about 15 minutes. Add the onion, garlic, shallots, and spinach and mix thoroughly.

Now, add the heavy cream little by little, then season to taste with the salt and pepper. Cover and continue cooking gently, stirring occasionally, for about 30 minutes, or until the excess moisture and flour taste diminish. Serve out in ramekins. *Serves 4-6.*

Note: This dish can be served as a vegetable or as a "Florentine" garnish for other dishes such as the Trout Mousse Florentine with Shrimp Sauce. In that case, cool the Creamed Spinach before using in the preparation with the trout.

FLORENTINE SPINACH

2 tbsp. butter
1 small onion, chopped
½ tbsp. chopped garlic
2 lb. fresh chopped spinach,
   drained
2 tbsp. Herbsaint
¼ cup white wine

½ cup strong chicken stock
Salt to taste
White pepper to taste
½ tsp. Tabasco sauce
¼ cup butter
¼ cup flour

Sauté the onions in the butter until clear. Add the garlic, spinach, Herbsaint, white wine, and chicken stock and mix thoroughly. Simmer for 30 minutes, stirring occasionally. Season to taste with the salt, white pepper, and Tabasco sauce.

In a separate small saucepan, heat the butter, blend in the flour, and cook this "roux" for five minutes, stirring often. Add the roux to the spinach mixture and blend thoroughly. Cook another 10 minutes. Remove from the stove and allow to cool. Grind very fine in a food processor. Reheat, adjust seasonings if desired, and serve. *Serves 6-8.*

This dish is best served with veal filet or Crabmeat Versailles.

RED CABBAGE ("ROTKOHL")

1 head red cabbage, approximately 1 to 1½ lb.
½ cup red wine vinegar
½ tsp. cinnamon
½ tsp. ground cloves
¼ tsp. ground nutmeg
2 bay leaves
⅓ cup sugar
2 tsp. salt

½ tsp. white pepper
1 medium yellow onion, thinly
   sliced
½ cup vegetable oil or bacon fat
1 large apple, peeled, cored,
   and sliced
Water or red wine
1 medium-sized white potato,
   peeled and grated

Wash the cabbage. Quarter the head and strip off and discard the outer leaves. Cut out and discard the core. Slicing at an angle, finely cut the quarters.

In a large bowl mix the vinegar, cinnamon, cloves, nutmeg, bay leaves, sugar, salt, and white pepper. Add the cabbage and toss. Cover the bowl with a towel and marinate overnight in the refrigerator.

In a saucepan, cook the sliced onion in vegetable oil until tender. Add the apple, marinated cabbage, and enough water or red wine to just cover the cabbage. Bring to a boil, lower the heat, cover, and simmer for 45 minutes to 1 hour. Stir in the potato. Cook until the juice is thick and syrupy, about 15 minutes, and serve. *Serves 6.*

This cabbage dish dish is served with game, beef rolls, and smoked pork loin.

SAUTEED CABBAGE FLAVORED WITH CARAWAY SEED

1 small whole cabbage	**½ cup chicken broth**
1 small yellow onion, sliced	**½ tsp. caraway seed**
1 tbsp. corn oil	**Salt to taste**
1 cup white wine	**White pepper to taste**

Slice and core the cabbage. Sauté the yellow onion in a skillet with the corn oil. When the onion is limp, add the cabbage, white wine, chicken broth, and caraway seed. Season to taste with the salt and white pepper. Cook until tender, about 20 minutes. *Serves 6.*

SAUERKRAUT

2 16-oz. jars sauerkraut	**1 tbsp. sugar**
½ lb. bacon	**Salt to taste**
⅛ cup cooking oil	**White pepper to taste**
1 large onion, sliced	**⅛ cup white vinegar**
2 8-oz. cans chicken broth	**½ cup applesauce**
3 bay leaves	**1 large, peeled potato**
½ tsp. caraway seeds	

Rinse the sauerkraut, drain and hold aside.

Cut the bacon into small strips and sauté in the oil until crisp. Add the sliced onion to the crisp bacon and sauté until the onions are limp.

Add the sauerkraut, chicken broth, bay leaves, caraway seeds, and sugar and cook for 45 minutes or until done. Season with the salt, white pepper, and vinegar.

Add the applesauce and grate the potato into the kraut. Slowly cook for another 5 minutes or until the potato and applesauce are mixed into the sauerkraut. *Serves 6-8.*

CARMELIZED ONION TART

4 bacon slices, chopped	White pepper, freshly ground,
3 tbsp. butter	to taste
4 lb. onions, thinly sliced	½ 1-lb. box frozen puff pastry,
Salt to taste	thawed

Heat a large, heavy skillet over medium heat and cook the chopped bacon until it is beginning to crisp, about 6 minutes.

Lower the heat a bit and add the butter and sliced onions. Cover the pan and cook the onions until they are brown and "caramelized," about 1 hour. Season with the salt and white pepper.

Roll out the puff pastry into a 13-inch diameter circle. Roll the pastry onto your rolling pin and unroll over a buttered tart pan with an 11-inch diameter and a removable bottom. Fit the pastry snugly into the sides and bottom of the pan. Trim off the excess pastry. Cover the pastry with a cloth and place in the freezer for thirty minutes. Preheat the oven to 425 degrees.

Remove the pastry from the freezer and fill it with the caramelized onions. Bake in the preheated oven until the crust is golden, about 30 minutes. Cool the tart slightly, cut into slices, and serve. *Serves 6.*

Note: The caramelized onions can be prepared a day ahead and stored covered in the refrigerator.

POTATO DUMPLINGS ("KARTOFFELKLOSSE")

3 medium-sized baking potatoes, peeled and quartered
Enough salted water to cover
potatoes
1/8 tsp. ground nutmeg
2 egg yolks

1 tbsp. chopped fresh parsley
Salt to taste
White pepper to taste
¼ cup all-purpose flour
More salted water

Boil the potatoes in salted water until very tender. Drain the water, cover the pan, and return to moderate heat to evaporate all the liquid from the potatoes. Transfer to a mixing bowl and mash. Cool in the refrigerator, then add the nutmeg, egg yolks, and parsley. Mix well. Season to taste with salt and white pepper.

Gradually work in the flour until the dough forms a ball. Place on a floured surface, roll, and shape into a long roll. Cut the roll into 2-inch lengths.

Drop the dumplings into boiling salted water. Cook until the dumplings float to the surface. Reduce the liquid to a gentle simmer and cook for 15 minutes. Remove the dumplings with a slotted spoon, drain, and serve immediately. *Serves 6.*

These dumplings are served with game and beef rolls.

DUCHESS POTATOES

4 medium potatoes, peeled and
quartered
Enough water to cover potatoes
1 tsp. salt
2 whole eggs

1 egg yolk
Pinch nutmeg
Salt to taste
White pepper to taste
2 tbsp. milk

Preheat the oven to 450 degrees.

Cover the potatoes with about an inch of water, season with the teaspoon of salt, and bring them to a boil in a covered saucepan. Steam them until the potatoes are tender, about 20 minutes. Drain the potatoes and mash them until they are smooth.

Beat the eggs and egg yolk together and whisk them into the potatoes. Season with the nutmeg, salt, and white pepper. Spoon the potato mixture into a pastry bag and pipe them around coquilles or ramekins for a garniture. Paint with the milk and bake in the preheated oven until lightly browned. *Serves 4.*

Use in Saint Jacques dishes and other seafood preparations.

LOUISIANA SWEET POTATO HASHBROWNS

2 medium egg yolks	¾ tsp. ground nutmeg
3 cups peeled, coarsely grated Louisiana sweet potato (2 large potatoes)	½ tsp. salt
	¼ tsp. white pepper
	3 tbsp. chopped parsley
1½ tbsp. flour	3 tbsp. cooking oil or margarine

In a bowl, beat the egg yolks lightly and add the grated sweet potato, flour, nutmeg, salt, white pepper, and chopped parsley. Fold together until all of the ingredients are well blended.

Heat the oil or margarine in a skillet. Drop the mixture by spoonfuls, keeping to a silver-dollar size and cook gently until browned around the edges. Flip each cake over and cook for 2-3 minutes. Remove to paper towels or napkins to drain. Keep warm. *Serves 6.*

This preparation goes well with filet of beef and game dishes.

RED-SKINNED POTATO SALAD

4 large, waxy red-skinned potatoes, cleaned
Enough water to cover potatoes
2 tbsp. salt, to add to the water
1½ tbsp. olive oil
1 leek, tough green tops
removed, finely sliced
⅓ cup chopped onion
⅓ cup coarsely chopped parsley

3 tbsp. coarsely chopped
chervil
1 tsp. minced garlic
¼ cup olive oil
2 tbsp. Dijon mustard
2 tbsp. white wine
1¼ tbsp. red wine vinegar
½ tsp. salt
¾ tsp. freshly ground black
pepper

Boil the potatoes in the salted water until they can be pierced fairly easily with the blade of a small knife, approximately 30 minutes. Drain and cool the potatoes at room temperature until they are cool enough to handle, yet still tepid. Cut the potatoes crosswise into ⅛-inch rounds, leaving the skin on.

Heat the 1½ tablespoons of olive oil in a skillet and sauté the leek for 1½ minutes. Transfer the leek to a bowl and add the onion, parsley, chervil, and garlic. Stir in the ¼ cup olive oil, Dijon mustard, white wine, and red wine vinegar. Season to taste with the salt and freshly ground black pepper.

Stir the mixture well, add the cooked, sliced red-skinned potatoes, and toss gently, making sure that the potato slices are well coated with the mixture, and serve. *Serves 6.*

Note: Red-skinned potatoes absorb the dressing better than baking potatoes. If red-skinned potatoes are not available, any other potato can be used in their place. New potatoes are particularly good.

TASSO RICE PILAF

¼ cup butter
6 tbsp. finely diced onion
2 cups rice

¾ cup tasso, diced
4 cups hot chicken stock
Salt and white pepper

Preheat the oven to 350 degrees.

In a heavy saucepan, melt the butter and sauté the diced onion until soft. Add the rice and tasso and stir and cook for 2 or 3 minutes. Add the hot chicken stock and bring to a boil. Tightly cover the pan and place it in the oven. Bake for 18-20 minutes.

To serve, fluff the rice in a bowl, season to taste with the salt and white pepper, and keep warm until ready to serve. *Serves 6.*

COLD WHITE BEAN SALAD

1 lb. dried white beans
12 cups chicken stock
2 cloves garlic, minced
½ cup minced yellow onion
½ cup olive oil
2 tbsp. fresh lemon juice

½ cup chopped fresh basil
1 cup diced red onion
1 large tomato, peeled, seeded, and diced
Salt to taste
Black pepper to taste

Rinse and pick over the beans. Cook them in the chicken stock with the minced garlic and yellow onion until they are done, about 2 hours. Cool.

In a large bowl, mix the beans with the olive oil, lemon juice, basil, red onion, and tomato. Season to taste with the salt and black pepper. Cover and refrigerate overnight. *Serves 6.*

Sauces and Dressings

FRESH DILL MAYONNAISE

1 cup mayonnaise
½ cup white wine
¼ cup chopped fresh dill (no stems)

2 tsp. Dijon Mustard
2 tsp. Worcestershire sauce
Salt to taste
White pepper to taste

Combine the mayonnaise with the white wine. Mix in the dill, Dijon mustard, and Worcestershire sauce. Season to taste with salt and white pepper. Transfer to a covered container and refrigerate overnight. *Makes 1¾ cups.*

Serve with gravlox or jellied salmon terrine, or other cold seafood and vegetable dishes.

BASIL PESTO MAYONNAISE

½ cup mayonnaise
1½ oz. (3 tbsp.) fresh basil leaves

2 tsp. pine nutes
1½ tsp. grated Parmesan cheese

In a food processor container, combine all of the ingredients and process until smooth. Transfer to a small covered container and and refrigerate until ready for use. *Makes ¾ cup.*

BASIL HOLLANDAISE

3 large egg yolks, room temper-
    ature
¼ cup white wine
1 tbsp. lemon juice
Salt to taste

3 large fresh basil leaves,
    chopped
White pepper to taste
½ cup clarified butter, warm

Combine yolks, wine, lemon juice, basil, salt, and pepper in a steel bowl. Whisk very briefly over a medium fire until the mixture forms a heavy ribbon. Remove from the fire. Stabilize the bowl on a towel and whisk in the warm clarified butter a little at a time. Adjust the salt and pepper if desired. Hold aside warm. *Makes 1 cup.*

Note: The usual method is to cook over or in hot water. You can achieve the same result directly over the heat or low flame. Just whisk faster and more thoroughly, being sure to rotate (spin) the bowl as you go, and also moving it to and from the heat to keep the bowl or mixture from becoming too hot, which will scramble in the egg yolks. The advantage is 5 minutes over the stove as opposed to 10 minutes in a double boiler.

BEARNAISE SAUCE

½ cup white wine
2 tbsp. tarragon vinegar
1 tbsp. minced shallots
2 black peppercorns, crushed

1 tbsp. chopped parsley
1 tbsp. chopped tarragon
3 egg yolks
¾ cup clarified butter

Cook the first 6 ingredients over direct heat until reduced by half. Strain and let cool. Then, whisking constantly in a double boiler or over hot water, add the egg yolks and cook until the mixture begins to thicken. Remove from heat while still whisking constantly.

Add the clarified butter a little at a time, whisking constantly. After all of the butter is added, adjust the seasonings. Serve in a sauce boat. *Makes 1½ cups.*

Use with seafood, poultry, and meats.

BECHAMEL SAUCE

2 tbsp. butter
1 small yellow onion, diced
1 small bay leaf
2 tbsp. flour
½ cup warm chicken stock

1 cup warm scalded milk
Salt to taste
White pepper to taste
Pinch ground nutmeg

In a saucepan, melt the butter and add the onions and bay leaf. Sauté for about 3 minutes or until the onions are soft but not yet beginning to color.

Whisk in the flour and cook for 1 minute. Add the warm chicken stock and warm milk. Bring to a gentle boil while whisking continuously to prevent lumps. Lower the heat to a simmer and reduce by half. Add the salt, pepper, and nutmeg to taste. Strain and chill until ready for use. *Makes ¾ cup.*

Use with vegetables, seafood, poultry, and veal.

BEURRE BLANC

1½ tbsp. butter
1 tbsp. flour
2 tbsp. boiling water
1 large egg yolk beaten with 1
   tbsp. water

6 tbsp. butter, cut into four
   pieces
Salt to taste
White pepper to taste

In a small saucepan, melt the butter. Stir in the flour, mix together, and cook for 2 minutes. Whisk in the boiling water and, while whisking vigorously, add the egg yolk/water mixture.

Add one at a time, stirring constantly over low heat, the butter cut into four pieces. Do not let the sauce come to a simmer; it will separate.

Season the sauce to taste with the salt and white pepper, strain, and serve immediately. *Makes approximately ¾ cup.*

Beurre Blanc is best served with seafood and poultry dishes or over vegetables.

BROWN SAUCE #1

½ cup vegetable oil
10 lb. veal knuckle bones, chopped into 3- to 4-inch pieces
3 large tomatoes, skinned and rough chopped
3 large onions, skinned and rough chopped
6 ribs celery, rough chopped
6 bay leaves
1 cup tomato paste
1½ gallons water
1 l. (slightly more than 1 qt.) red wine
Salt and freshly ground black pepper

Heat the oil in a braising pan. Add the veal bones and brown on all sides.

Add the tomatoes, onions, celery, and bay leaves. Brown the vegetables. Stir in the tomato paste and transfer the contents of the braising pan to a soup or stock pot. Add the water and the red wine. Season lightly with salt and black pepper. Bring the contents to a boil, turn down to a slight simmer, and cook for 6-8 hours.

Strain the sauce and reduce the remaining liquid to 1½ gallons. *Makes 1½ gallons.*

Note: This sauce can be used as is with meats or as a base for other sauces such as Demi-glace and Brown Tomato Sauce. It freezes well and should be done up in manageable, small freezer-bag portions to be used when needed.

BROWN SAUCE #2

6 tbsp. butter
1 cup finely chopped onions
1 cup finely chopped carrots
½ cup flour
1 cup red wine
¼ cup finely chopped parsley
1 tsp. dried thyme leaves
1 bay leaf
2 tbsp. tomato paste
5 cups beef or veal stock, or bouillon
Salt and freshly ground black pepper to taste

Melt the butter in a saucepan and add the onion and carrot. Cook over a moderate heat until the vegetables are somewhat browned.

Stir in the flour and cook, stirring frequently, until the mixture has browned.

Carefully whisk in the red wine and let it boil up. Add the parsley, thyme, bay leaf, and tomato paste. Whisk in the stock or bouillon a little at a time until it is all added and the liquid is smooth. Bring to a boil, turn down to a simmer, and reduce by half. Season to taste with salt, if necessary, and freshly ground black pepper. *Makes 3 cups.*

This is a base sauce to which ingredients are added to make other dark sauces for meats and poultry.

DEMI-GLACE SAUCE #1

3 tbsp. arrowroot   1½ gallons Brown Sauce #1, hot
½ fifth bottle port wine

Mix the arrowroot together with the port wine. Whisk the mixture into the hot Brown Sauce #1. Simmer and reduce to one gallon, about 30 minutes. *Makes 1 gallon.*

As with the Brown Sauce, this sauce freezes well. Serve with meat and poultry dishes.

DEMI-GLACE SAUCE #2

2 cups Brown Sauce #2   2 tbsp. brandy
2 cups meat stock   Salt and pepper

Pass the Brown Sauce through a fine strainer. Combine the strained Brown Sauce with the meat stock and brandy. Bring to a boil, reduce to a simmer, and reduce to 2 cups. Season with salt and pepper if desired. *Makes 2 cups.*

Use for meats and poultry.

GLACE DE VIANDE

1½ gallons Brown Sauce #1, hot   ½ fifth bottle port wine

In a saucepan, combine the hot Brown Sauce #1 and port wine. Simmer until reduced to 1 quart. *Makes 1 quart.*

As with the Demi-glace Sauce, this sauce freezes well. Serve with meat and poultry dishes, or as a base for other sauces.

MARCHAND DE VIN SAUCE

2 cups Demi-glace Sauce #2   ¼ cup pureed garlic cloves
1 cup pureed fresh mushrooms   Salt and freshly ground black
1 cup pureed onion   pepper

Combine the Demi-glace Sauce with the pureed mushrooms, onion, and garlic. Bring to a boil, reduce to a simmer, and reduce in half. Season with salt and pepper to taste. *Makes 2 cups.*

Use for meats, especially beef.

CAFE DE PARIS BUTTER

½ cup butter
1 small egg yolk
½ tsp. finely chopped shallots
¼ tsp. finely chopped anchovy
¼ tsp. finely chopped sage
¼ tsp. finely chopped garlic
½ tsp. finely chopped parsley

¼ tsp. dry mustard
½ tsp. lemon juice
¼ tsp. finely chopped tarragon
¼ tsp. coarse black pepper
¼ tsp. paprika
¼ tsp. curry powder
¼ tsp. finely chopped thyme

Soften the butter in a bowl. Fold in the egg yolk. Fold all the seasoning ingredients together well with the butter and egg yolk. Transfer to a covered container and refrigerate until stiff.

The butter can be put into cups or molds before it is refrigerated.

It is served by the slice or spoonful, cold, on simple grilled veal chops or steaks, and other meats, and melts from the heat of the steak. *Makes a good ½ cup.*

Serve with grilled veal chops or steaks.

CARPACCIO SAUCE

1 cup Dijon mustard
⅓ cup olive oil
1½ tbsp. minced parsley

3 tbsp. freshly squeezed lemon
  juice

In a small bowl, combine the Dijon mustard with the olive oil, lemon juice, and parsley. Transfer to a lidded container or jar and store refrigerated for 24-48 hours before use. *Makes 1½ cups.*

Use with Tuna or Salmon Carpaccio.

CRABMEAT STUFFING FOR MUSHROOMS, SHRIMP, AND CRABCAKES

½ cup butter
1 bunch green onions, chopped
1 small yellow onion, chopped
1 cup heavy cream
½ cup white wine
1 cup bread crumbs
¼ cup lemon juice
½ lb. white crabmeat
Salt to taste
White pepper to taste

Melt the butter in a sauté pan and sauté the chopped green onions and yellow onion just until they soften. Add the heavy cream and white wine, bring to a boil, turn down to a simmer, and cook for a few minutes until the liquids reduce somewhat and begin to thicken.

Fold in the bread crumbs and the lemon juice. Continue simmering until the mixture forms a mass that can be shaped. Carefully fold in the white crabmeat, season to taste with the salt and white pepper, and remove from the heat. *Makes approximately 3 cups.*

Use to stuff mushrooms or shrimp, or in crabcakes.

CREOLE SEASONING (BROUSSARD'S PEPPER)

½ cup paprika
2 tbsp. cayenne pepper
2 tbsp. garlic powder
½ tsp. dried whole thyme leaves
½ tsp. dried tarragon, crumbled
½ tsp. dried basil, crumbled
¼ tsp. salt
½ tsp. black pepper

Combine all of the ingredients in a bowl and mix well. Store in an airtight container. *Makes ¾ cup.*

Use to season foods as they are being prepared.

CREOLE MUSTARD DRESSING (HORSERADISH CREOLE MUSTARD CREAM)

¾ cup sour cream
⅓ cup prepared horseradish
2 tbsp. Creole mustard

2 tbsp. heavy cream
½ tsp. salt or to taste
¼ tsp. white pepper or to taste

In a small mixing bowl, combine the sour cream with the prepared horseradish, Creole mustard, and heavy cream. Blend thoroughly. Season the mixture with the salt and white pepper. Transfer to a lidded container or jar and refrigerate until ready for use. *Makes 1⅓ cups.*

Serve with Daube Glace and other Creole dishes.

CREOLE MUSTARD-CAPER SAUCE

1 tbsp. butter
1 tbsp. minced shallots
3 oz. capers, drained
1½ tbsp. caper liquid

8 oz. heavy cream
3 oz. (6 tbsp.) Creole mustard
Salt and pepper to taste

In a heavy saucepan, melt the butter. Add the shallots and capers and sauté. Deglaze the pan with the caper liquid. Add the heavy cream. Bring to a boil, reduce heat, and simmer for about 5 minutes. Whisk in the Creole mustard and simmer for another 3-4 minutes. Adjust the salt and pepper and keep warm. *Makes 1¼ cups.*

Goes well with veal and poultry dishes.

CREOLE TOMATO SAUCE

1 tbsp. olive oil
½ small yellow onion, diced
¼ medium sweet green bell
    pepper, diced
1 tsp. minced garlic
3 tbsp. tomato paste
3 cups diced Creole tomatoes or
    other ripe tomatoes

2 cups veal or chicken stock
½ cup Sauterne wine or any
    sweet white wine
Salt to taste
Black pepper to taste
1 tbsp. arrowroot, dissolved in
    1 tbsp. wine or water
2 tbsp. butter

Heat the olive oil in a sauté pan and sauté the onion, bell pepper, and garlic until soft. Do not let them brown. Add the tomato paste and cook for 5 minutes. Add the tomatoes and stock, bring to a boil, and cook for 20 minutes. Pass the mixture through a strainer, pressing to get as much of the pulp as possible into the sauce. Discard the debris left in the strainer and return the sauce to the pan.

Add the wine, bring to a light boil, and reduce by half. Season to taste with the salt and pepper. Stir in the arrowroot mixture and butter and continue cooking for 2 minutes more to thicken. Remove the pan from the heat and keep warm. *Makes approximately 2½ cups.*

Note: The thickening property of arrowroot varies from bottle to bottle. You may need a little more than the recipe calls for, but rarely less.

The method of using arrowroot is like using cornstarch. Arrowroot, however, results in a more transparent and liquid state that is more conducive to a sauce as opposed to a gravy. It also requires very little cooking time.

This sauce is used with seafood and poultry.

TOMATO SAUCE

2 cups Brown Sauce #2
2 cups diced, seeded, skinned
  tomatoes

2 tbsp. tomato paste, or to taste
1 clove garlic, pressed
Salt and pepper

Pass the Brown Sauce #2 through a fine strainer.

Combine the strained Brown Sauce with the tomato, tomato paste, and pressed garlic clove. Bring to a boil, reduce to a simmer, and reduce to three cups. Season with salt and pepper if desired. *Makes 3 cups.*

Use for meats, poultry, and fish.

DIABLE SAUCE

1 tbsp. butter
2 tbsp. sliced green onions
1 tbsp. minced shallots
½ cup white wine

Degreased pan juices
Green peppercorns to taste
½ cup Brown Sauce #2

Heat the butter in a saucepan and gently sauté the sliced green onions and shallots until clear. Add the white wine and pan juices (from birds or roast for which you are preparing this sauce) with green peppercorns to your taste; reduce by half. Add the Brown Sauce #2 and reduce by a fourth. Salt to taste. *Makes approximately 1½ cups.*

This sauce can be served with Cornish game hens, quail, and duckling.

DORE SAUCE

2 cups peeled and deveined
  shrimp
¼ cup green onions
1 tbsp. chopped shallots
1 tbsp. chopped garlic
1 cup mushrooms
1 cup crawfish tail meat

2 tbsp. lemon juice
Salt
White pepper
½ cup cream
¼ lb. butter
1 cup jumbo lump crabmeat

In a skillet cook shrimp with very little water until ½ to ¾ done, drain. Add next 9 ingredients, mix well, and bring to a good simmer. Stir in the butter to emulsify, then add the lump crabmeat. Keep warm but do not boil. *Serves 6.*

Serve over sauteed, broiled, or grilled fish.

HORSERADISH SOUBISE

1 tbsp. butter
¼ cup finely minced onion
1 oz. (2 tbsp.) white wine

10 oz. sour cream
1 cup horseradish

Melt the butter in a heavy saucepan, add the onion and sauté until lightly colored. Add the wine and reduce until almost completely evaporated. Add the sour cream and simmer gently for 5 minutes. Add the horseradish and mix well. Keep warm. *Makes 2 cups.*

Serve with seafood.

FENNEL-PIMENTO VINAIGRETTE

½ cup diced fennel, bulb only
½ cup chopped dill pickles
½ cup chopped pimentos
2 tbsp. chopped shallots
2 tbsp. chopped parsley
½ tbsp. chopped garlic

1 cup salad oil (do not use olive oil)
½ cup red wine vinegar
Salt to taste
Black pepper to taste

In a bowl, combine the fennel with the pickles, pimentos, shallots, parsley, and garlic. Mix well. Stir in the salad oil and red wine vinegar and season to taste with the salt and black pepper. Transfer to a covered container and refrigerate until ready for use. *Makes approximately 2½ cups.*

Used with seafood and vegetable dishes.

FINANCIERE SAUCE

¼ lb. butter
1 clove garlic, chopped
2 dry shallots, chopped
1 whole chopped green onion

12 black olives, pitted and sliced
1 cup sliced mushrooms
2 tbsp. port wine
1 cup Demi-glace Sauce

In a skillet, melt the butter and sauté the chopped garlic, shallots, and green onion for 2-3 minutes. Add the olives, mushrooms, port wine, and Demi-glace Sauce. Simmer for 5 minutes.

Hold aside warm until ready for use, or transfer to a covered container or jar and refrigerate. Sauce will keep for a week. *Makes 2 cups.*

Serve with sweetbreads, meats, and fowl.

GRAVLOX SAUCE

½ cup mayonnaise
¾ cup heavy cream
1½ tbsp. fresh dill

½ tsp. salt, or to taste
¼ tsp. freshly ground black
  pepper, or to taste

In a small bowl, beat the mayonnaise together with the heavy cream. Stir in the fresh dill and season with the salt and freshly ground black pepper. Transfer to a lidded container or jar and store refrigerated for 24-48 hours before use. *Makes approximately 1¼ cups.*

Use with Tuna or Salmon Carpaccio.

GREEN PEPPERCORN SAUCE ("SAUCE AU POIVRE VERTE")

3 tbsp. minced carrot
2 tbsp. minced onion
1 tbsp. minced celery
2 bay leaves
½ tsp. dried leaf thyme
1 cup white wine
1 cup wine vinegar

2 cups Demi-glace Sauce #1
1 cup heavy cream
½ cup green peppercorns
Liquid from green peppercorns
  to taste
Salt

Put the minced carrot, onion, and celery into a saucepan. Add the bay leaves, thyme, white wine, and vinegar and reduce by half. Then add the Demi-glace Sauce #1 and the heavy cream and reduce to the desired consistency. Strain the sauce. Add the whole green peppercorns, the packing liquid to taste, and season with the salt. *Makes 3 cups.*

Use with seafood or meats.

GREEN REMOULADE SAUCE

½ cup sour cream
⅓ cup heavy cream
⅓ cup prepared horseradish
1 tbsp. minced parsley
1½ tsp. minced green onion
1½ tsp. minced celery

1½ tsp. minced green bell pepper
1 tsp. Dijon mustard
½ tsp. freshly squeezed lime juice

In a small bowl, beat the sour cream together with the heavy cream until well blended. Fold in the horseradish, parsley, green onion, celery, bell pepper, Dijon mustard, and freshly squeezed lime juice. Transfer to a covered container and refrigerate overnight, or until well chilled. *Makes a good 1⅓ cups.*

Serve with cold boiled seafood and cold vegetables.

GRENOBLOISE SAUCE

½ lb. butter
1 clove garlic, chopped
1 dry shallot, chopped
1 whole green onion, chopped
3 sliced cornichons

2 tbsp. capers
1 tbsp. lemon juice, or to taste
Salt
White pepper

Melt the butter in a saucepan with the chopped garlic, shallot, and green onion. Bring to a simmer and add the cornichons, capers, and lemon juice. Season to taste with salt and white pepper. Hold aside warm. *Makes approximately 1⅓ cups.*

Grenobloise Sauce is used with sweetbreads, seafood, poultry, and veal.

LEMON BASIL SAUCE

1 tbsp. butter
1 tbsp. minced shallots
¼ cup chopped fresh basil

¼ cup white wine
2 tbsp. fresh lemon juice
10 oz. (1¼ cups) heavy cream

In a heavy saucepan, melt the butter and sauté the shallots and basil. Remove shallots and basil to the side.

Deglaze the pan with the white wine and lemon juice. Reduce until almost all of the liquid is evaporated. Add the heavy cream and reduce until the sauce coats a spoon. Strain the sauce and put the basil and shallots in a blender with a small amount of the sauce and puree. Return the puree to the sauce and mix well. *Makes 1 cup.*

Serve with seafood.

MORNAY SAUCE

1 cup reduced fish, shellfish, or
   chicken stock
2 cups Béchamel Sauce
2 egg yolks

¼ cup heavy cream
½ cup grated Parmesan cheese
½ cup grated Gruyère cheese
2 tbsp. butter

Combine the stock with the Béchamel Sauce and simmer for about 10 minutes.

In a bowl, beat the egg yolks together with the heavy cream. Whisk some of the sauce into the egg yolk-cream mixture then whisk back into the saucepan with the remaining sauce. Fold in the cheese and finish with the butter. Allow the cheese to melt, but do not allow the sauce to come to a simmer—it will separate.

Mornay Sauce is usually served over the dish, then the dish is placed under the broiler to brown. Serve immediately with fish, eggs, poultry, or veal dishes. *Makes 3 cups.*

ORANGE COGNAC AND PORT WINE SAUCE

¼ cup Grand Marnier, Curacao, or other orange brandy
¼ cup port wine
2 cups rich Brown Sauce #2 or Demi-glace Sauce #1

Salt
Black pepper

Combine the brandy, port wine, and rich Brown Sauce #2 or Demi-glace Sauce #1 in a saucepan and simmer for 15 minutes. Season to taste with the salt and black pepper. *Makes approximately 2 cups.*

Serve this sauce with duck, quail, or stuffed game hen.

PESTO SAUCE

1¾ cups green onions, green part only, sliced
¾ cup olive oil
¼ cup chopped fresh basil

2 small cloves garlic
1½ tbsp. toasted almond slivers
3 tbsp. grated Parmesan cheese

Combine the green onions, olive oil, basil, garlic, and almonds in a blender container. Process until smooth. Transfer to a covered bowl, fold in the grated Parmesan cheese, and refrigerate until ready for use. *Makes approximately 2½ cups.*

Use with seafood and pasta dishes.

PORT SAUCE

½ tbsp. butter
3 tbsp. minced shallots
1 cup port wine

4 cups Demi-glace Sauce #1
2 tbsp. butter at room temperature

In a heavy saucepan, melt ½ tbsp. butter and sauté the shallots. Add the port wine and reduce by half. Add the Demi-glace Sauce #1, simmer, and reduce by half. Remove from the heat and whip in the soft butter. Pass through a fine strainer and keep warm until ready to serve. *Makes 2¼ cups.*

Serve with veal, beef, lamb, and pork.

RAVIGOTE SAUCE

1 cup real mayonnaise
¾ tbsp. minced green bell pepper
¾ tbsp. minced green onion
¾ tbsp. minced anchovy fillets
¾ tbsp. minced pimento

½ tsp. minced fresh tarragon
¼ tsp. freshly squeezed lemon juice
Salt to taste
White pepper to taste

In a small mixing bowl, combine the mayonnaise with the green bell pepper, green onion, anchovies, pimento, tarragon, and lemon juice. Fold all of the ingredients together until well blended. Season to taste with the salt and white pepper. Transfer to a lidded container and keep refrigerated until ready for use. *Makes 1¼ cups.*

Serve with cold boiled seafood, boiled eggs, and cold cooked or raw vegetables.

RAW TOMATO-BASIL SAUCE

4 ripe medium tomatoes,
  skinned, seeded, and
  chopped
1 medium red onion, finely
  chopped
2 cloves garlic, minced

3 tbsp. finely chopped fresh
  basil leaves
3 tbsp. finely chopped parsley
2 tbsp. olive oil
1 tsp. salt
¼ tsp. black pepper

In a bowl, combine the tomatoes with the red onion and garlic. Add the chopped basil, parsley, olive oil, salt, and black pepper. Adjust the seasonings if desired. Cover the bowl and refrigerate overnight if possible, or until ready for use. *Makes 2 cups.*

Use with vegetable dishes.

RED CURRANT SAUCE

½ cup raisins
1½ cups port wine
1 tsp. powdered mustard
¼ tsp. ground ginger
¼ tsp. ground clove
2 tsp. grated lemon zest

2 tsp. grated orange zest
2 tsp. cornstarch
¼ cup orange juice
2 tbsp. lemon juice
¼ cup currant jelly
Salt and white pepper to taste

Combine the raisins in a saucepan with the port, mustard, ginger, clove, and the zests of the lemon and orange. Bring to a boil and simmer for 5 minutes.

Mix the cornstarch together with the orange juice and whisk the mixture into the sauce. Add the lemon juice and currant jelly. Bring to a simmer and cook for 2 minutes more. Season with salt and white pepper. *Makes 1¾ cups.*

This sauce can be served hot or cold. It will become jellylike when chilled. The sauce is served with venison, game, and lamb, as well as with pâtés and terrines.

RED ONION CONFIT

2 tbsp. butter
3 red onions, thinly sliced
¼ cup red wine

½ cup currant jelly
Salt to taste
Black Pepper to taste

Heat the butter in a sauté pan and sauté the sliced red onions until they become limp. Add the red wine and currant jelly. Reduce until the consistency approaches that of a marmalade. Season with salt and pepper to taste. Transfer the Red Onion Confit to a covered container and refrigerate overnight. *Makes approximately 1½ cups.*

Serve with Boudin Blanc Terrine.

RED REMOULADE SAUCE

½ cup Creole mustard
2 tbsp. ketchup
2 tbsp. corn oil
1 tbsp. minced yellow onion
1 tbsp. minced green onion
1 tbsp. minced celery
1 tsp. minced parsley

1 tsp. prepared horseradish
1 tsp. paprika
½ tsp. sugar
¼ tsp. pressed garlic
¼ tsp. Worcestershire sauce
¼ tsp. white pepper

In a small mixing bowl, whisk the Creole mustard and ketchup together and then whisk in the corn oil. Stir in the yellow onion, green onion, celery, parsley, and prepared horseradish. Add the paprika, sugar, garlic, Worcestershire sauce, and white pepper. Whisk all together until well blended. Transfer to a covered container and refrigerate overnight, or until well chilled. *Makes 1 cup.*

Served with boiled shrimp, crabmeat, eggs, or cold vegetables.

ROASTED RED PEPPER AND DILL CREAM

1 14-oz. can whole red pimentos, drained
½ cup heavy cream

8 oz. cream cheese
1 tsp. salt
2 tbsp. fresh dill

In a blender container, combine the red pimentos with the heavy cream, cream cheese, and salt. Blend into an homogenous mixture. Transfer the mixture to a container, fold in the fresh dill, cover, and refrigerate overnight. *Makes enough topping for 1 cake.*

ROSEMARY-MINT FOND

2 tbsp. butter
3 tbsp. fresh rosemary, chopped
 fine
4 tbsp. fresh mint, chopped
 fine

2 tbsp. minced shallots
½ cup red wine
2¼ cups Demi-glace Sauce #1
Salt and freshly cracked pepper
 to taste

In a heavy saucepan, melt the butter and sauté the rosemary, mint, and shallots for about 4 minutes. Deglaze the pan with red wine and reduce by half. Add the Demi-glace Sauce and bring to a boil. Reduce the heat and simmer until the sauce coats the back of a spoon. Adjust the seasoning and keep warm until ready to use. *Makes 2 cups.*

Use with lamb, pork, and beef.

SHITAKE-CABERNET SAUCE

2 tbsp. butter
1 chopped dry shallot
1 cup sliced fresh or rehydrated
  shitake mushrooms

¼ cup cabernet wine
1 cup Demi-glace Sauce
Salt to taste
Black pepper to taste

Melt the butter in a saucepan and briefly sauté the chopped shallot and mushrooms. Add the cabernet wine and bring to a boil. Add the Demi-glace Sauce, season to taste with the salt and black pepper, cover, and simmer gently for 10 minutes. Hold aside warm. *Makes approximately 2 cups.*

Serve with dark meats and duck.

SWEET TOMATO AND SPICY SHRIMP RELISH

½ cup olive oil
4 tbsp. minced dry shallots
4 cloves garlic, minced
4½ cups tomato, peeled, cored,
  seeded, and chopped
2 cups sugar

2 cups red wine vinegar
1 tsp. salt
1½ tsp. ground white pepper
¼ lb. cold, spicy, boiled, shelled
  shrimp, chopped

Heat the olive oil in a heavy saucepan. Add the shallots and garlic and sauté for about 3-4 minutes. Add the tomato and sauté for another 2 minutes.

Next add the sugar, red wine vinegar, salt, and white pepper and mix well. Bring to a boil, then reduce heat to a simmer. Cook mixture about 15 minutes or until most of the liquid has reduced. Let cool to room temperature and refrigerate. When mixture is cold, fold in the shrimp and refrigerate overnight. *Makes 1 quart.*

Serve with other seafood, especially fillets of fish.

ROUILLE

¼ tsp. saffron threads
3 garlic cloves, pressed
1 cup mayonnaise

2 tsp. fresh lemon juice, or to
  taste
Cayenne pepper to taste

If you have a mortar and pestle, it is best to make the rouille using them. If not, you will need a small sturdy crockery or metal bowl. Crumble the saffron threads into the mortar or bowl. Add the pressed garlic. Work together to make a smooth paste. Work in the lemon juice and then the mayonnaise. Season to taste with cayenne pepper. Transfer to a tightly capped jar and store in the refrigerator until ready for use. *Makes approximately ⅔ cup.*

Serve the Rouille with seafood, seafood soups and stews, and poultry. It is the traditional sauce/flavorant for Bouillabaisse.

SHRIMP SAUCE

¼ lb. fresh butter
½ cup flour
1 cup sliced green onions
2 shallots, chopped fine
2 garlic cloves, chopped fine
2 bay leaves
1 tbsp. leaf thyme

2 tbsp. paprika
2 lb. peeled and deveined
  shrimp (your preferred size)
½ cup white wine
1½ cups heavy cream
Salt to taste
White Pepper to taste

Melt the butter in a saucepan, blend in the flour, and cook this "roux" gently, about 15 minutes. Add the green onions, shallots, garlic, bay leaves, leaf thyme, paprika, and shrimp. Cook approximately 5-6 minutes, add the white wine and cream slowly, allowing the sauce to thicken as you go. Add the salt and white pepper to taste, simmer for 10 minutes more, and serve as directed. *Serves 6-8.*

This sauce is used with Trout Mousse Florentine with Shrimp Sauce. It can be used with any fish dish, and even with poultry or veal dishes.

TARRAGON SAUCE

1 tbsp. butter
½ cup minced shallots
½ cup fresh minced tarragon

½ cup red wine
2 cups Demi-glace Sauce #2
3 tbsp. soft butter

In a heavy saucepan melt the butter and saute the shallots and tarragon. Deglaze the pan with red wine and reduce. Add the Demi-glace Sauce #2. Simmer for about 10-15 minutes or until the sauce coats the spoon. Remove from heat and whip in the soft butter. Keep warm. *Makes 2 cups.*

Served with veal, beef, or lamb.

THREE-PEPPER RELISH

1 cup chopped green onions
1 small red bell pepper, cut into
  ½-inch-by-2-inch strips
1 small black bell pepper, cut
  into ½-inch-by-2-inch strips
1 small yellow bell pepper, cut
  into ½-inch-by-2-inch strips
1 cup cider vinegar

¼ cup chopped garlic
½ cup brown sugar
½ tsp. allspice
1 tsp. mustard seed
¼ tsp. black pepper
¼ tsp. ground cinnamon
1 tsp. minced fresh ginger
1 tbsp. dried currants

Combine the green onions, red, black, and yellow bell peppers in a saucepan. Stir in the cider vinegar and add the garlic, brown sugar, allspice, mustard seed, black pepper, ground cinnamon, fresh ginger, and dried currants. Cover the pot and bring the liquids to a boil. Lower the heat to a gentle simmer and cook for about 45 minutes, or until the liquids are almost completely reduced. Store in a covered container in the refrigerator. *Makes approximately 2 cups.*

WARM REMOULADE SAUCE

2 tsp. butter
3 tbsp. finely minced yellow
   onion

¼ cup white wine
1 cup sour cream
4 tbsp. prepared horseradish

Melt the butter in a heavy saucepan. Add the yellow onion and sauté until lightly colored. Add the white wine and reduce until almost completely evaporated. Then add the sour cream and simmer gently for 5 minutes. Add horseradish and mix well. Keep warm. *Makes 1¼ cups.*

Used in seafood dishes.

WHITE WINE CREAM SAUCE

1 cup pan drippings from
   roasted or sautéed fowl, or
   chicken broth
¼ cup white wine
¼ cup heavy cream

1 tsp. minced shallots
1 tsp. minced garlic
1 tsp. minced green onions
4 tbsp. butter, cut in 3 pieces

Reduce drippings or broth for 5 minutes over high heat. Degrease the sauce and add wine. Reduce briefly and add the cream, shallots, garlic, and green onions and simmer for 5 minutes. Remove from the heat and swirl in the butter to finish sauce. *Makes approximately 1¼ cups.*

Serve with roasted or sautéed fowl.

CREOLE VINAIGRETTE DRESSING

¼ cup chopped green onions
¼ cup chopped cornichon
  pickles
¼ cup chopped pimento
1 tbsp. chopped shallots
1 tbsp. chopped parsley
1 tbsp. capers

1 tsp. chopped garlic
1 cup salad oil (do not use olive
  oil)
½ cup red wine vinegar
Salt to taste
White pepper to taste

Combine the ingredients in a jar or shaker of some sort and shake vigorously until all is well blended. Store the vinaigrette in a jar or tightly capped container in the refrigerator until ready for use. When ready for use, shake the dressing again to blend the ingredients. *Makes approximately 2 cups.*

BROUSSARD'S HOUSE DRESSING

1 cup mayonnaise
¼ cup Creole mustard
1 tbsp. minced celery
1 tbsp. minced bell pepper
1 tbsp. minced white onion

1 tbsp. minced green onion
1 tsp. Worcestershire sauce
1 tsp. white vinegar
Salt to taste
White pepper to taste

Combine the mayonnaise and mustard then fold in the celery, bell pepper, white onion, and green onions. Stir in the Worcestershire sauce and the vinegar. Season to taste with salt and white pepper. Transfer the dressing to a covered container and refrigerate until ready for use. *Makes 1½ cups.*

CAESAR SALAD DRESSING

¼ cup lemon juice
1 tbsp. Dijon mustard
1 tsp. Worcestershire sauce
½ tsp. Coleman's dry mustard
2 anchovy fillets, chopped

1 tsp. chopped garlic
2 whole eggs
1 cup olive oil
Salt to taste
White pepper to taste

In a blender container, combine the lemon juice with the Dijon mustard, Worcestershire sauce, mustard, anchovy fillets, and garlic. Process until smooth.

Add the eggs and turn the blender on low. While the blender is on, add the olive oil, very slowly, in a thin stream, until it is all completely incorporated into the mixture and the dressing is emulsified. Season to taste with salt and white pepper. Transfer the Caesar Salad Dressing to a covered container or jar and refrigerate until ready for use. *Makes approximately 2 cups.*

BUTTERMILK BLUE CHEESE DRESSING

1 cup buttermilk
½ cup mayonnaise
1 tbsp. chopped white onion
1 tsp. chopped garlic
1 tsp. green peppercorns,
    drained

¼ tsp. dried thyme leaves
3 tbsp. well crumbled blue
    cheese
Salt to taste
White pepper to taste

In a bowl, combine the buttermilk and mayonnaise, whisking them until they are well blended.

In a blender container, combine the white onion, garlic, peppercorns, and thyme leaves. Pour in enough of the buttermilk and mayonnaise to cover; puree.

Fold this mixture into the bowl ingredients along with the crumbled blue cheese. Season to taste with salt and white pepper. Transfer to a covered container in the refrigerator until ready for use. *Makes approximately 1¾ cups.*

ORANGE MAYONNAISE DRESSING

1 cup mayonnaise
½ cup fresh orange juice
1 tbsp. Worcestershire sauce
½ tbsp. French Brandy

Sugar to taste
Salt to taste
White pepper to taste

Combine all of the ingredients, transfer to a covered container, and refrigerate until well chilled. Serve over Belgium Endive, radiccio, or any "bitter" type salad green. *Makes 1½ cups.*

Note: The fresh orange juice can be replaced with 1 ounce (2 tablespoons) of concentrate.

Seafood

CREOLE POT AU FEU

BROTH

2 tbsp. olive oil
1 large onion, roughly chopped
2 medium carrots, roughly chopped
2 sticks celery, roughly chopped
1 small sweet green bell pepper, seeded and chopped
1 small sweet red bell pepper, seeded and chopped
1 dozen fresh okra pods, sliced
2 leeks (white part only), thinly sliced
2 tbsp. tomato paste
2 medium-sized tomatoes, peeled, seeded, and diced
1 cup brandy
½ cup white wine
½ cup Herbsaint
2 tbsp. filé powder, or to taste
3 qt. seafood or chicken stock

Begin the Pot au Feu by making the broth. Heat the olive oil in a large saucepan or soup pot. Sauté the onion, carrots, celery, green and red bell peppers, and leeks. Add the okra pods. When the vegetables are nearly transparent, stir in the tomato paste and tomatoes and cook briefly.

Being very careful, add the brandy and ignite it to burn out the alcohol and flavor the cooking vegetables. Add the white wine and Herbsaint. Season with the filé powder to taste. Then add the seafood or chicken stock and simmer until vegetables are cooked.

POT AU FEU

½ cup white wine
1 tbsp. chopped dry shallots
1 tbsp. chopped garlic
½ lb. boned, skinned pompano fillet, cut into bite-sized pieces
½ lb. boned, skinned trout fillet, cut into bite-sized pieces
1 lb. peeled, deveined raw shrimp
1 dozen raw oysters
½ lb. crawfish tail meat
½ lb. jumbo lump crabmeat, warmed
6 whole boiled crawfish for garnish
2 tbsp. chopped parsley

In a separate soup pot, combine the white wine with the chopped shallots and garlic and add the pompano, trout, shrimp, oysters, and crawfish tail meat. When the seafood is half cooked, add the previously made broth and simmer until done.

To serve, mound the seafood and vegetables in center of each of 6 bowls, surround with the broth, garnish with the warmed jumbo lump crabmeat and a whole boiled crawfish, sprinkle with chopped parsley, and serve. *Serves 6.*

Note: "Filé" powder is a thickening, coloring, and flavoring agent. It is actually ground sassafras leaves and comes to New Orleans cuisine from the Louisiana Indian.

SHRIMP CREOLE

4 tbsp. butter
3 large onions, rough chopped
2 large bell peppers, seeded and rough chopped
1 stalk celery, minced
4 cloves garlic, minced
5 large tomatoes, skinned, seeded, and rough chopped
1 tsp. thyme
4 bay leaves
1 tsp. paprika

2 tbsp. minced parsley
Salt and white pepper to taste
¼ tsp. cayenne pepper, or to taste
1 tsp. cornstarch
1 tbsp. water
3 lb. whole raw shrimp, headed, peeled, and deveined
4 cups hot cooked rice

In a wide heavy skillet, melt the butter and sauté the onions, bell pepper, celery, and garlic until all becomes limp, about 3-5 minutes. Add the tomatoes, thyme, bay leaves, paprika, parsley, salt, pepper, and cayenne pepper. Simmer together for 10 minutes.

Mix the cornstarch with the water and blend into the sauce. Bring to a simmer and cook for 2 minutes, then add the shrimp. Let the shrimp remain in the sauce for just 3-5 minutes, or until they are cooked but not overcooked. Spoon the Shrimp Creole onto plates and top with a scoop of rice. *Serves 6.*

SHRIMP CURRY

3 tbsp. butter
2 lb. preferred size shrimp,
   peeled and deveined
2 tbsp. green onions, sliced
1 tbsp. shallots, chopped
1 tbsp. parsley, chopped
2 tbsp. curry powder, or to taste
1½ tbsp. applesauce

1 tsp. diced red pimento
1 tbsp. chutney
2 tbsp. hearts of palm, sliced
3 tbsp. sherry wine
2 cups heavy cream
Salt to taste
Chutney

Melt the butter in a saucepan and add the shrimp, green onions, shallots, parsley, and curry powder. Cook for 3-4 minutes.

Add the applesauce, pimento, chutney, hearts of palm, and sherry wine. Add the cream slowly and salt to taste. Simmer for 10-12 minutes and serve. Serve additional chutney on the side. *Serves 4.*

PESTO GRILLED SHRIMP WITH THREE-PEPPER RELISH AND TASSO PILAF

3 dozen 10-15 count shrimp,
   peeled and butterflied
6 wood or metal skewers
Pesto Sauce as marinade

Tasso Pilaf, warmed
About 2 cups Three-Pepper
   Relish, warmed

Skewer six shrimp each on six skewers and marinate overnight in the Pesto Sauce in a covered container in the refrigerator.

To cook the shrimp, grill on them medium heat, turning once, being careful not to overcook or burn them.

Mold the Tasso Pilaf in a small ramekin and place in the center of the plates. Place the grilled shrimp in a standing position around the pilaf and spoon the Three-Pepper Relish over them. *Serves 6.*

Note: "Tasso" is a cured, highly seasoned beef that is used in Louisiana cooking as a flavoring meat.

SHELLFISH ST. JACQUES

2 tbsp. butter
8 oz. medium or small peeled, deveined shrimp
¼ cup sliced green onions
1 tbsp. chopped garlic
1 tbsp. chopped shallots
½ cup sauterne or other non-dry white wine
2 cups heavy cream
8 oz. crawfish tail meat

6 oz. lump crabmeat
2 cups sliced mushrooms
Salt to taste
White pepper to taste
About 3 cups mashed potatoes as garnish
3 tbsp. butter
Parmesan cheese, as garnish, to taste

Preheat the oven to 400 degrees.

In a wide skillet, heat the butter and sauté the shrimp until half-cooked. Add the green onions, garlic, and shallots, mix thoroughly, and cook another 2-3 minutes without browning. Add the sauterne or white wine, reduce by half, and add the heavy cream. Continue cooking over medium heat until the sauce has thickened.

Add the crawfish tails, lump crabmeat, and sliced mushrooms and continue cooking only long enough for all to become well heated. Season to taste with the salt and white pepper. Hold aside warm until ready for use.

Using a pastry bag with a fluted tip, border individual baking dishes or some coquille-type shells with mashed potatoes to which you have blended the butter. Place seafood mixture in dishes, top with the Parmesan cheese, and bake in the preheated oven until hot and bubbly. Serve immediately. *Serves 6.*

FILE GUMBO
WITH SHRIMP, OKRA, AND SAUSAGE

2 lb. whole shrimp
10 cups water
2 tsp. salt
½ cup butter
½ cup flour
1 large white onion, chopped
1 bunch green onions, chopped
½ cup chopped celery
1½ cups sliced fresh okra (or 1
  10-oz. pkg. frozen)
1 tbsp. minced parsley

1 lb. andouille sausage (or any
  spicy smoked sausage available)
3 crabs, top shells and lungs
  removed
1 tsp. black pepper
½ tsp. cayenne pepper
Salt to taste
1 rounded tbsp. filé powder
4 cups hot cooked rice

Before cooking the shrimp, peel, head, and devein them, reserv-ing the shells as well as the meat. Put the water, salt, and shrimp peels and heads into a soup pot and bring to a boil. Continue boiling for approximately 45 minutes, or until the water has been reduced to about 3 cups. Strain out the shells and reserve the liquid. Set aside.

Melt the butter in a large soup pot and add the flour. Cook while stirring until the mixture, the "roux," becomes a mahogany-brown color. Add the white onions, green onions, celery, and okra. Continue cooking until the vegetables brown. Add the parsley and sliced sausage and cook for about 5 minutes.

Blend the reserved shrimp liquor into the ingredients, bring to a boil, reduce to a simmer, and add the crabs, black pepper, cayenne pepper, and salt. Cover and simmer gently for 1 hour. Add the shrimp and cook for 2 minutes more. Blend in the filé powder. To serve, put ½ cup hot, cooked rice into each of 6 large soup bowls and ladle the gumbo into each bowl. *Serves 6-8.*

TROUT CHAPON

½ cup chopped green onions
2 tbsp. dry shallots
1 small clove garlic, chopped
2 dozen 21-25 count, raw peeled shrimp
½ cup chopped mushrooms
1 tbsp. chopped fresh dill

¼ cup dry vermouth
6 5-6 oz. trout fillets, skinned
1 cup heavy cream
6 tbsp. butter
Salt
White pepper
½ tsp. lemon juice

Preheat the oven to 350 degrees.

Using a wide skillet, combine the green onions, shallots, garlic, shrimp, mushrooms, dill, and vermouth. Warm the skillet on the range top and then fold in the trout fillets so that they are well covered with the seasoning ingredients. Cover the skillet with foil and cook in the preheated oven for about 10 minutes, or until the trout is just cooked. Carefully remove the trout fillets and the shrimp from the skillet, making sure that the seasoning ingredients remain in the skillet. Hold the trout and shrimp aside warm.

Return the skillet to the stove top and reduce the liquids in half. Add the cream and butter and season with the salt, white pepper, and lemon juice. Simmer for 5-10 minutes. Serve the trout and shrimp with the sauce spooned over. *Serves 6.*

FILLET OF TROUT MARCUS

6 6-oz. trout fillets
Salt
White pepper
Lemon juice
All-purpose flour

5 whole eggs, beaten
¾ cup clarified margarine
Marcus Garnish
2 tbsp. chopped parsley

Season the trout fillets with the salt, white pepper, and lemon juice. Dredge them in the flour; shake off any excess. Dip the floured fillets in the beaten eggs, then sauté them in hot clarified margarine until the edges begin to brown. Turn the fish over and cook gently until it flakes easily, about 5 minutes.

Serve the trout with the Marcus garnish spooned over them, garnished with chopped parsley.

MARCUS GARNISH

6 fresh, trimmed and cooked artichoke bottoms; or 1 14-oz. can artichoke bottoms
2 tbsp. sliced green onions
½ tsp. chopped garlic
½ tsp. chopped dry shallots
3 tbsp. "nonpareil" capers, or other select small capers, rinsed
½ cup white wine
½ cup fresh lemon juice
1 cup fresh butter
Salt to taste
White pepper to taste

In a saucepan, combine the artichoke bottoms with the green onions, garlic, shallots, capers, white wine, and lemon juice. Bring to a boil. Divide the butter into three pieces and add all at once. Swirl and agitate in the pan until the butter is fully emulsified. Season to taste with the salt and white pepper.

Do not let the sauce overheat at this point, not even to a simmer. If the sauce simmers, the butter with separate and the sauce will thin out. The sauce needs to remain creamy from the butter. *Serves 6.*

I created this dish for my younger son, Marcus Preuss.

TROUT MOUSSE FLORENTINE WITH SHRIMP SAUCE

2 lb. fresh trout fillets
4-5 egg whites
1½ tsp. salt
⅓ tsp. white pepper
1 tsp. nutmeg

5 cups heavy cream
Creamed Spinach
Shrimp Sauce
1 tbsp. chopped parsley

Preheat the oven 350 degrees.

Cut the trout fillets in small pieces and run through a food chopper until very fine, all the while adding the egg whites, salt, white pepper, and nutmeg. When mixed and chopped fine, add the heavy cream, about a cup at a time, allowing for a thorough blend between additions.

Butter the inside of a ring mold lightly, fill the bottom third of the mold compactly with the mousse. With a pastry bag, pipe the spinach in a circle around the mold, keeping it within the center of the mousse. Finish filling the mold with mousse and pack tightly again, keeping the spinach in the center. Place mold in a pan of hot water (¾ the way up the mold) and bake in the preheated oven for 25 or 30 minutes. A toothpick inserted in the center will come out clean when done. Allow the mousse to sit 5-6 minutes before unmolding.

To serve, invert the mold on a platter to free the mousse, then fill the center of the ring with the Shrimp Sauce. Also, coat the mousse with the sauce, sprinkle with chopped parsley, and serve. Carve at tableside and pass the extra sauce. *Serves 6-8.*

TROUT NOUVELLE ORLEANS

2 tbsp. butter
¼ cup vegetable oil
Salt and pepper to taste
6 6-8 oz. trout fillets

¾ cup flour
1½ cups Tomato-Shrimp Relish
¾ cup Lemon Basil Sauce

Melt butter in a heavy skillet with the vegetable oil. Salt and pepper the trout and dust with the flour. Cook in the hot butter-oil mixture on both sides until cooked, about 6 minutes. Drain the fillets and place on warm serving plates. Top each fillet with 4 tablespoons of the Tomato-Shrimp Relish and spoon 2 tablespoons of the Lemon-Basil Sauce around each fish. *Serves 6.*

POACHED TROUT WITH TOMATOES AND ARTICHOKES

6 6-oz. trout fillets	3 medium tomatoes
3 tbsp. butter	9 artichoke hearts
3 tbsp. sliced green onions	2 cups red wine
1 tbsp. chopped dry shallots	2 cups Brown Sauce #2
1 tsp. chopped garlic	4 tbsp. butter

Preheat oven to 375 degrees.

Cut the fish fillets in half lengthwise and roll them into "paupiettes," pinwheel fashion.

Melt the butter in an ovenproof pan, then add the green onions, shallots, and garlic. Place the twelve paupiettes in the pan and cover with buttered wax paper. Bake until done, about 15-20 minutes. Meanwhile peel, seed, and cut the tomatoes into 6 wedges each. Cut the artichoke hearts into quarters.

Remove the fish from the skillet and keep warm. To the remaining pan juices add the red wine and Brown Sauce #2, the tomato wedges, and the artichoke hearts. Heat thoroughly. To finish, add the butter and warm, while stirring, until the butter is melted, but still emulsified. Pour sauce and garniture over each serving. *Serves 6.*

FLOUNDER PONTCHARTRAIN
WITH FENNEL-PIMENTO VINAIGRETTE

1 dozen 2-3 oz. flounder fillets
Salt
White pepper for seasoning
Crabcake recipe mixture (from
    Louisiana Crabcakes with
    Creole Mustard-Caper
    Sauce), final cooking not yet
    done

2 tbsp. Creole Seasoning or
    Broussard's Pepper
1 cup poaching liquid (½ cup
    white wine and ½ cup water)
Salt to taste
Black pepper to taste
2½ cups Fennel-Pimento Vinai-
    grette

Preheat the oven to 400 degrees.

Lay the flounder fillets on a board and pound them gently until they will fold. Season them lightly with salt and white pepper.

Divide the crabcake mixture evenly into a dozen balls and wrap a seasoned flounder fillet around each ball. Secure the fillets for cooking with a toothpick. Place fillets in a shallow baking dish and sprinkle with the Creole Seasoning. Pour in the poaching liquid, cover with parchment paper, and bake in the preheated oven for 15 minutes. Place on a warm serving plate, remove toothpicks, and pour Fennel-Pimento Vinaigrette over the top. *Serves 6.*

REDFISH HERBSAINT

½ cup Herbsaint liquor
¾ cup white wine
1 tbsp. finely chopped shallots
¼ cup julienned carrots
¼ cup julienned celery
¼ cup julienned leek, white
    part only
6 fresh mushroom caps, stems
    removed

6 4-oz. redfish fillet pieces
1½ cups heavy cream
Salt to taste
White pepper to taste
3 lemons, juiced
¾ lb. lump crabmeat
¾ cup butter
Herbsaint to taste

In a sauté pan, combine the Herbsaint, white wine, shallots, carrots, celery, leeks, and mushroom caps. Add the redfish fillets and poach on low heat for approximately 8-10 minutes, or until the flesh is firm but not dry. Remove the fish from the pan and set on a dinner plate. Hold aside warm.

Increase the heat and reduce the poaching liquid by half. Add the cream and reduce by half again. Season to taste with salt, white pepper, and lemon juice. Reduce to a simmer and add the crabmeat. Toss until it is heated through. Finish the sauce by swirling in the butter and splashing in a small amount of Herbsaint. Serve the sauce immediately over the warm fish. *Serves 6.*

Note: Herbsaint is a New Orleans version of Pernod, or Pastis. Bass or pompano can be used in place of the redfish.

POMPANO NAPOLEON

6 6-oz. pompano fillets
12 large scallops, cleaned
6 pieces puff pastry, 3-inch
   rounds

1¼ cups Creole Mustard-Caper
   Sauce
4 tbsp. Broussard's Pepper

Cut pompano fillets in half lengthwise and pound gently with the flat of a large kitchen knife. Wrap one piece of pompano around each scallop and secure with a toothpick. Sprinkle with Broussard's Pepper and grill or broil.

Split puff pastry rounds in half and place bottom on warm plate. Place cooked pompano-scallops on each side and top with Creole Mustard-Caper Sauce. Place puff pastry top over each serving. *Serves 6.*

Note: If you can't find puff pastry sheets to make your own rounds, inquire at your local pastry shop.

FILLETS OF POMPANO WITH ORANGES

Zest from 2 oranges, julienned
Water to cover zests
2 tbsp. butter
1 tsp. shallots, finely chopped
8 3-oz. fillets of pompano, seasoned with salt

½ cup fish stock
Juice from ½ lemon
Juice from of 2 oranges
1 cup heavy cream
½ cup sherry or Madeira (optional)

Parboil the orange zests in the water for a few minutes and drain. Melt the butter in a shallow pan and add shallots. Arrange the seasoned pompano in the pan. Add fish stock and the lemon and orange juices. Spread the drained julienned orange peel on top of the fish.

Cover the fish with a circle of wax or buttered paper cut the size of the pan, with a small hole in the center. Bring to a boil, cover the pan, and cook for 10-12 minutes. Remove the fish to a heated serving dish. Cook the liquid in the pan until it is reduced to half of the original quantity and add the heavy cream. Bring back to a boil and add, if desired, sherry or Madeira. Strain the sauce over the fish, replacing the orange peel that falls off. Serve 2 fillets per portion with the sauce spooned over. *Serves 4.*

POMPANO VERMOUTH

1 tsp. minced garlic
1 tsp. minced shallots
1 tbsp. sliced green onions
½ cup raw, peeled, deveined shrimp
½ cup dry vermouth

6 6-8 oz. skinless pompano fillets (folded once, head to tail)
Salt and white pepper to taste
¾ cup heavy cream
1 cup lump crabmeat

Preheat the oven to 400 degrees.

In an ovenproof skillet place the garlic, shallots, green onions, shrimp, vermouth, and pompano fillets. Season with salt and white pepper. Cover with foil and cook in a hot oven approximately 20 minutes. Remove pompano to heated plates and keep warm.

To the pan juices add the heavy cream and reduce on top of the stove until it begins to thicken. Add the crabmeat and heat thoroughly. Spoon the crabmeat sauce over the pompano fillets and serve. *Serves 6.*

POACHED POMPANO WITH TRUFFLES

6 8-oz. pompano fillets
Salt and white pepper to taste
1 cup white wine
½ cup sauterne wine
¼ cup truffle shavings

2 cups heavy cream
1 cup fine julienne of onions,
   carrots, and celery
4 tbsp. fresh butter

Preheat the oven to 400 degrees.

Fold the pompano fillets over and place in a shallow pan. Season with salt and pepper to taste and add the white wine, sauterne, and truffle shavings. Cover loosely with foil and poach in the preheated oven until cooked, about 15 minutes.

Transfer fish to warm plates, then reduce remaining liquid by three-fourths. Add the cream and reduce by half. Add the julienned vegetables, adjust salt and pepper, bring to a boil, finish with fresh butter, pour over fish, and serve. *Serves 6.*

SOLE MORNAY

6 6-oz. sole or flounder fillets
Salt and white pepper
1½ cups dry white wine
1 bay leaf
1 tbsp. minced dry shallot

Butter to grease ovenproof
   dishes
3 cups Mornay Sauce
¾ cup grated Gruyère cheese

Season the sole fillets with salt and white pepper.

Heat the wine in a wide skillet with the bay leaf and shallot. When it boils, add the sole, cover the fish with a piece of parchment or foil, and then cover the pan. Cook for about 5 minutes, or until the fish are done. Carefully transfer the cooked fillets to warm, buttered ovenproof dishes.

Reduce the remaining liquids by half. Then whisk the reduced liquids into the Mornay Sauce and nap the fillets. Sprinkle with the Gruyère cheese and place the dishes under a broiler to melt the cheese and lightly brown the sauce. Serve immediately. *Serves 6.*

FILLETS OF SOLE WITH WHITE GRAPES

1 tbsp. butter
½ small onion or 2 shallots,
    finely chopped
8 3-oz. sole fillets, seasoned to
    taste with salt and pepper
½ cup white wine
½ cup water

½ cup heavy cream
1 egg yolk
2 tbsp. butter
1 cup seedless white (green)
    grapes
2 tbsp. cream, whipped

Spread the tablespoon of butter in a shallow pan and sprinkle with the onion or shallots. Roll up the seasoned fillets, skewer with toothpicks and arrange them in a pan. Add the white wine and the water. Cover with a circle of wax or buttered paper cut the size of the pan with a small hole in the middle. Bring to a boil. Cover the pan with its top and cook 10-12 minutes. Remove the fish to a heatproof dish and remove the toothpicks.

Cook the liquid until it is reduced to about ½ cup and add the heavy cream. Reduce and whisk together with the egg yolk and butter. Cook just until the butter is melted: do not boil!

Simmer the seedless grapes in a little water for a few minutes, drain, and place them around the fish. Fold the whipped cream into the sauce and pour it over the fish. Brown under a hot broiler flame. Serve two per person. *Serves 4.*

DOVER SOLE FILLETS
WITH SALMON SOUFFLE

½ lb. boneless salmon fillet,
  diced
3 egg whites
1 tsp. salt
¼ tsp. white pepper
¼ tsp. ground nutmeg
2 cups heavy cream
6 4-oz. Dover sole fillets

2 tbsp. fresh butter to grease
  the baking pan
1 cup Chablis wine
2 cups heavy cream
Dash of lemon juice
1 tbsp. fresh butter
Salt and white pepper to taste
1 tbsp. chopped parsley

Preheat the oven to 400 degrees.

In a food processor grind the salmon fillet very fine, adding the egg whites gradually. When well blended, add the salt, pepper, and nutmeg. Then while mixing, add the heavy cream, ½ cup at a time, and continue to mix thoroughly until well blended. Chill.

Butter a shallow baking pan, lay the sole fillets flat, and, by means of a pastry bag fitted with a fluted tip, pipe some of the salmon souffle on top of each fillet in a decorative fashion. Alternatively, you can roll up or fold over the fillets and stuff them with the salmon mixture. Pour white wine into the pan, loosely cover with foil, and bake in the preheated oven about 12-15 minutes, or until the salmon mixture is firm but fluffy to the touch. Remove the sole fillets to warm plates, reduce the cooking liquid by half, add the additional cream, and reduce to the desired consistency. Add a dash of lemon juice, salt and pepper to taste, and finish with the fresh butter. Pour over each portion of sole, sprinkle chopped parsley, and serve. *Serves 6.*

PECAN-STUFFED SALMON

6 5-6 oz. salmon fillets
4 cups fine bread crumbs
4 cups pecan pieces
2 cups chopped parsley
2 cups chopped green onion
½ cup lemon zest

1 cup lemon juice
4 cups softened butter
Salt to taste
Black pepper to taste
Cayenne pepper to taste

Preheat the oven to 400 degrees.

Prepare the salmon fillets for stuffing by cutting each down the middle, but only halfway through, and from the middle cut into the sides to form a pocket. Cover and hold aside.

In a bowl, combine the bread crumbs, pecan pieces, parsley, green onions, lemon zest, and lemon juice. Fold in the softened butter and season to taste with the salt, black pepper, and cayenne pepper. Stuff the mixture into the prepared salmon fillets.

Place the stuffed fillets in a buttered baking pan and roast in the preheated oven for about 10 minutes, or until the salmon is cooked to your liking. *Serves 6.*

SALMON DE LA SALLE

2 dozen plum tomatoes,
  skinned
3 sweet green bell peppers,
  seeded and rough chopped
3 cucumbers, seeded and rough
  chopped
2 medium white onions, rough
  chopped
1 clove garlic
2 cups tomato juice
1 tbsp. chopped parsley
1 cup olive oil

4 lemons, juiced
Salt to taste
Black pepper to taste
Tabasco sauce to taste
Cumin to taste
½ tbsp. corn oil
2 dozen 1-oz. salmon fillet
  slices
1½ dozen thin lemon slices for
  garnish
Parsley sprigs for garnish

In a food processor of blender container, combine the tomatoes, green bell peppers, cucumbers, onions, garlic, tomato juice, and parsley. Stir in the olive oil and lemon juice. Pulse the processor or blender to achieve a chopped, not pureed, mixture. Season to taste with the salt, black pepper, Tabasco sauce, and cumin. Spoon the mixture onto serving plates.

In a hot skillet, heat the corn oil and sear the slices of salmon on both sides and place four pieces on top of each sauced plate. Garnish with the lemon slices and parsley sprigs. *Serves 6.*

POACHED SALMON ARGENTEUIL

6 5-6 oz. salmon fillet pieces
6 fresh artichoke bottoms

2 dozen asparagus
2 cups white wine

SAUCE

2 cups heavy cream
Juice from 1 lemon
½ cup butter
2 tbsp. chopped fresh basil

Salt and white pepper to taste
12 oz. lump crabmeat
Basil leaves for garnish

Preheat the oven to 400 degrees.

Fold each fish fillet in half over four asparagus and set on an artichoke bottom. Arrange them in an ovenproof skillet and pour the white wine over them. Cover loosely with the foil and bake in the preheated oven for about 15 minutes. Remove each fillet portion to a warm plate and keep warm in the oven.

To the remaining liquids in the pan, to make the sauce, add the cream, lemon juice, butter, and basil. Over a moderate fire on the range top, reduce sauce until it thickens slightly. Add the crabmeat, season to taste with salt and white pepper, and allow it to heat thoroughly.

Serve the salmon with the crabmeat sauce spooned on top and garnished with fresh basil leaves. *Serves 6.*

OVEN-ROASTED SNAPPER FRITO MISTO

6 4-oz. snapper fillets
Salt and freshly ground black
    pepper to taste
1 cup white flour
3 cups eggwash
1 cup corn oil
6 large raw shrimp, peeled

6 raw oysters
6 raw scallops
1 cup corn flour
1¼ cups Warm Remoulade
    Sauce
2 cups Horseradish Soubise

Salt and pepper snapper fillets and dust with flour. Place in the eggwash for 3-4 minutes. In a heavy skillet, heat ½ cup of the oil. Sauté the snapper over medium heat until golden brown. Drain and keep warm.

While the snapper is cooking, salt and pepper the shrimp, oysters, and scallops. Dip in the eggwash and roll in the corn flour. Pour off the fish oil and heat the remaining ½ cup of oil in the same pan. Sauté the shrimp, oysters, and scallops. Drain.

Place the snapper on warm plates and arrange seafood on top. Pour 2 oz. (4 tablespoons) of the Horseradish Soubise over the seafood. Spoon the Warm Remoulade Sauce around the sides. *Serves 6.*

RED SNAPPER PIPERADE

½ onion, julienned
¾ bell pepper, julienned
1 clove garlic, minced
1 large ripe tomato, skinned,
    seeded, and chopped

2 tbsp. olive oil
8 oz. burgundy wine
1 tbsp. chopped fresh basil
Salt and white pepper to taste
2 8-oz. red snapper fillets

Preheat the oven to 350 degrees.

Sauté the onion, bell pepper, garlic, and tomato in olive oil until the vegetables are limp. Add the red wine and reduce until about 2 ounces of the wine remains. Add the fresh basil. Season to taste with salt and pepper. Season the fish with the salt and pepper and grill until about halfway cooked (about 2-3 minutes on a fast grill).

Place the fish in a baking pan, top with the vegetable sauce, and bake at 350 degrees until the liquids are absorbed. Serve with the vegetable sauce spooned on top. *Serves 2.*

SEA SCALLOPS WRAPPED IN FRESH LEEK

3 dozen large sea scallops
3 dozen green "ribbons" of
    fresh leek, blanched (white
    and green part, same width
    as scallops)
½ cup sauterne wine

6 tbsp. fresh butter to grease
    the pan
Salt and pepper to taste
1½ cups heavy cream
Dash lemon juice
2 tbsp. fresh butter

Preheat the oven to 400 degrees.

Take each scallop and wrap a ribbon of leek around it, just over-lapping the ends. Trim off the excess and secure with a toothpick.

Generously butter a cookie pan or solid broiler pan, place scallops on pan, and pour over sauterne wine. Season with salt and pepper to taste. Bake in the preheated oven 12-15 minutes, or until scallops are slightly firm to the touch. Place scallops on warm plates. Pour the cooking liquid into a small saucepan and reduce. Add the heavy cream and reduce further until desired it is the consistency. Add a dash of the lemon juice, taste for salt and pepper, and finish with fresh butter. Pour sauce around scallops and serve. *Serves 6.*

Poultry and Game

QUAIL LOUISIANA WITH FRESH SAGE AND GREEN ONION STUFFING

FRESH SAGE AND GREEN ONION STUFFING

2 cups strong chicken or game
  stock
1 bunch green onions, sliced
3 tbsp. chopped fresh sage
  leaves

1 tbsp. chopped garlic
Salt to taste
White pepper to taste
1 cup bread crumbs

Preheat the oven to 350 degrees.

In a skillet or saucepan, combine the chicken or game stock with the green onions, sage, and garlic and season with the salt and white pepper. Bring to a boil and simmer for 10-12 minutes. Remove from the heat.

Fold in the French bread crumbs, being sure there is enough to make a stuffing that is firm, yet moist. Allow to cool enough to handle.

QUAIL

12 partially boned quail
Corn oil

Salt
Black pepper

To cook the quail, stuff them with the dressing. Wipe them with a little corn oil and season lightly with salt and pepper. Place them in a roasting pan and into the preheated oven for 20-30 minutes, or until they are done. You can tell this by piercing through the breast with a skewer and pressing to see if the liquids run red. If not, the birds are done. Serve two per person with the pan juices sprinkled over. *Serves 6.*

QUAILS IN CRANBERRY SAUCE

½ cup butter
1 tbsp. finely chopped French
    shallots
1 tbsp. finely chopped green
    onions
1½ tsp. chopped fresh tarragon
1¼ cups bread crumbs
Salt to taste
White pepper to taste
1 dozen 2½-oz. boneless quails

12 slices bacon
3 tbsp. cranberries, fresh or
    frozen
½ cup brandy
1½ cups red wine
3 cups Brown Sauce #2
3 tbsp. finely chopped French
    shallots
3 tbsp. butter

Begin the preparation of this dish by first making the stuffing. In a sauté pan, melt the butter and sauté the shallots, green onions, and tarragon for 1 minute. Incorporate the bread crumbs into the mixture, taking care to distribute the butter and bread crumbs evenly. Season to taste with the salt and white pepper. Remove from the heat and hold aside until ready for use.

Preheat the oven to 350 degrees. Prepare the quail. The boneless quails should be split down the back; if not, do so. Spread the quails out, flesh side down. Spread the stuffing onto the interior of the boneless quails. Roll up and shape the quails into their original shape. With the legs sticking upwards, wrap the quails with bacon, and secure with toothpicks. Roast in a pan in the preheated oven for 25-30 minutes.

Make the sauce in the roasting pan. Remove the quails from the oven. Pour the excess oil out of the pan, add the cranberries, and stir them into the pan drippings. Deglaze and flambé with the brandy. Extinguish the flame with the red wine. Add the Brown Sauce #2 and shallots. Simmer for an additional 5 minutes. Finish the sauce by swirling in the additional butter. Arrange the quail, legs up, on a plate. Sauce the quails and serve. *Serves 6.*

QUAILS FORESTIERE

12 partially boned quails (split
    down the back, rib cage
    removed)
Fresh Sage and Onion Stuffing
12 strips bacon with 12 tooth-
    picks
1 cup Calvados or apple brandy

1 truffle, finely sliced
1 cup Brown Sauce #2
¾ cup heavy cream
Sauteed Cabbage Flavored
    with Caraway Seed
1½ tbsp. butter

Preheat the oven to 400-425 degrees.

Place the quails skin-side down and spoon on the stuffing, spreading it evenly over the breast areas. Fold skin from neck area over stuffing and fold left and right wings over and interlock them. Then, keeping the whole bird intact, fold over right thigh then left thigh over that, squeeze to maintain shape, and then wrap with a strip of bacon, going around from the thigh area over the neck cavity and back to the thigh area (leaving the breast exposed). Secure with a toothpick.

Roast quails, breast-side up in an appropriate skillet or saucepan at 400-425 degrees for about 25 minutes. Remove them from the oven, pour off the excess liquid, immediately add the Calvados, and loosen and remove quails.

To the saucepan add the sliced truffle, Brown Sauce #2, and cream. Mix well and return the quails, breast-side down to the sauce. Simmer this until the sauce is the desired consistency. Remove toothpicks, place two quails per serving on beds of prepared Sauteed Cabbage Flavored with Caraway Seed, finish the sauce with the butter, spoon over the quails, and serve. *Serves 6.*

BRAISED ABITA QUAILS WITH WHITE BEANS, RED CABBAGE, AND RED CURRANT SAUCE

12 dressed quail
Corn oil
Salt and white pepper

Cold White Bean Salad
Red Cabbage ("Rotkohl")
1¾ cups Red Currant Sauce

Preheat the oven to 350 degrees.

To cook the quail, wipe them with a little corn oil and season lightly with salt and pepper. Place them in a roasting pan and into the preheated oven for 20-30 minutes, or until they are done. You can tell this by piercing the breast with a skewer and pressing to see if the liquids run red. If not, the birds are done.

Plate the quails. First spoon some of the Cold White Bean Salad on the plate on one side and Red Cabbage on the other side. Place a quail in the center of each plate. Serve with the Red Currant Sauce spooned over the quail. *Serves 12.*

CORNISH HEN GRILLED DIABLE

6 rock cornish game hens
1 tbsp. Madagascar green peppercorns
Salt for seasoning

Black pepper for seasoning
6 tbsp. fresh butter
2 tbsp. chopped parsley
1½ cups Diable Sauce

Preheat the oven to 450 degrees.

Split the hens down the back, open up, and remove backbone and rib cage. Trim wing tips off. Place hens flat with skin-side up. Make incisions around the breasts and thighs and insert some crushed green peppercorns. Place hens on a flat roasting pan, skin-side up, season with salt and black pepper, and add a little fresh butter on each hen. Place in the preheated oven, immediately turning down to 350 degrees. Roast about 25-30 minutes, basting hens twice with their own juices during the cooking.

To serve, place golden brown hens on plates and sprinkle with chopped parsley. Serve Diable Sauce in a sauceboat, separately. *Serves 6.*

ROASTED CORNISH GAME HENS WITH SPINACH AND MUSHROOM STUFFING

SPINACH AND MUSHROOM STUFFING

3 tbsp. clarified butter
1¼ cups spinach, blanched and
   drained
3 cloves of garlic, minced
¾ lb. mushrooms, sliced

⅓ cup dry vermouth
⅓ cup cream
¾ cup bread crumbs, or more if
   needed

Heat the clarified butter in a sauté pan or skillet and add the spinach, garlic, mushrooms, and dry vermouth. Cook over high heat for 3 minutes, then add the cream and reduce by a third. Add the bread crumbs and cook until thick and moist. Allow to cool. *Makes approximately 3 cups.*

ROASTED CORNISH GAME HENS

6 boned Cornish hens
2 tsp. salt
1½ tsp. lemon juice
Spinach and Mushroom Stuffing

6 slices bacon
1¼ cups clarified butter
1¼ cups White Wine Cream
   Sauce

Preheat the oven to 450 degrees.
Lay the boned Cornish hens out flat, skin-side down, on a work surface. Season with the salt and lemon juice. Spoon about ½ cup Spinach and Mushroom Stuffing onto each bird and fold the hens up around the stuffing. Wrap each hen with a strip of bacon and secure the bacon and the closure of the hen with toothpicks.

Arrange the hens in a roasting pan, add the clarified butter, and roast in the preheated oven for 45 minutes. Add the pan drippings to complete the White Wine Cream Sauce and serve it on the side or over the birds. *Serves 6.*

DEMI-POULET VALLE DAUCHE

6 tbsp. butter
6 5-6 oz. chicken breasts
½ cup Calvados
¼ cup chopped green onions
1 clove chopped garlic
2 dry shallots, chopped

1 tsp. chopped fresh thyme
1 cup chopped mushrooms
1 cup heavy cream
Salt to taste
White pepper to taste

In a skillet, heat the butter and sauté the chicken breasts until they are done. Remove the chicken and hold aside warm.

Deglaze the pan with the Calvados. Add the green onions, garlic, shallots, fresh thyme, mushrooms, and heavy cream. Reduce until the sauce foams up. Return the chicken breasts to the pan, season with the salt and white pepper and simmer for two minutes longer. Serve with the sauce spooned over. *Serves 6.*

CHICKEN ST. CHARLES

6 4-5 oz. skinless chicken breast
   pieces
Salt
White pepper
1 tbsp. lemon juice
Fresh Sage and Green Onion
   Stuffing
½ cup chopped raw oysters

¾ cup flour
Eggwash, made with 1 egg and
   ½ cup milk
1 cup bread crumbs
¼ cup corn oil
¾ cup butter
2 tbsp. lemon juice, or to taste

Flatten the chicken breasts with a rolling pin or meat hammer. Season with the salt and pepper and sprinkle with the lemon juice. Fold the dressing together with the oysters. Place a heaping tablespoon of dressing on each breast and fold over. Secure the breasts with toothpicks if desired.

Roll in the flour, dip in the eggwash, and dredge in the bread crumbs. Sauté in the corn oil until the bread-crumb coating is golden brown. Keep hot.

In a small saucepan, melt the butter and add the lemon juice. Season with salt and white pepper to taste. Serve the sauce over the cooked, stuffed chicken breasts. *Serves 6.*

POUSSIN ROCHAMBEAU

6 poussin, semiboneless,
   weighing 12-14 oz.
4 tbsp. butter
2 tbsp. minced shallots
4 oz. fresh spinach, cleaned and
   chopped
6 oz. ground veal
6 oz. ground tasso

½ cup heavy cream
2 oz. plain bread crumbs
12 slices apple smoked bacon
2 tbsp. butter
3 cups sliced wild mushrooms
1½ cups Marchand de Vin
   Sauce
¾ cup Béarnaise Sauce

If poussin is unavailable, Cornish game hens can be used. Preheat the oven to 350 degrees.

Wash and dry poussin and set aside. In a heavy pan melt 4 tablespoons of the butter and sauté the shallots and spinach. Set aside to cool. In a large bowl, combine the ground veal, tasso, cooled spinach, heavy cream, and bread crumbs. Mix well. Make 6 small "meatballs" and stuff into poussin. Wrap 2 slices of bacon around base of each poussin using toothpicks to hold in place. Place poussin in a shallow roasting pan and cook for about 30 minutes.

In another heavy pan melt the additional butter and sauté the mushrooms. Divide the mushrooms on 6 heated plates and place poussin on the mushrooms. Top with 4 tablespoons of the Marchand de Vin Sauce and 2 tablespoons of the Béarnaise Sauce. *Serves 6.*

Note: A poussin is a young chicken. Tasso is a Louisiana cured-beef seasoning meat.

DUCKLING ANDREAS

3 3- to 3½-lb. ducklings
Salt
Black pepper
2 tbsp. fresh rosemary
1 14-oz. can Bing cherries,
   drained, juice reserved

2 tbsp. clarified butter
6 Poached Pears Madame
   Preuss
About 2 cups Orange Cognac
   and Port Wine Sauce

Preheat the oven to 350 degrees.

Season the ducklings inside and out with the salt, black pepper, and rosemary. Roast the ducklings for about 2½ hours. Remove the ducklings, split them in half with a French knife, and bone out backbone and rib cage. Deglaze the pan with the reserved cherry juice.

Sauté the Bing cherries in the clarified butter and spread over the pears. Arrange each pear on a plate with half of a duck. Spoon the deglazing liquid over the pears and serve the Orange Cognac and Port Wine Sauce over the ducks. *Serves 6.*

I created this dish for my older son, Andreas Preuss.

BONELESS DUCKLING NORMANDY

3 4-5 lb. ducks
4 tbsp. softened butter
Salt and freshly ground pepper
   to taste
3 tsp. dried thyme
3 small onions, quartered

3 cloves garlic, crushed
1 cup stock or red wine
3 cups Apple Shallot Mincemeat
¾ cup Marchand de Vin Sauce

Preheat oven to 450 degrees.

Wash ducks and dry inside and out. Cut wings off. Rub the softened butter on the outside of the ducks. Rub salt, pepper, and thyme into skin and cavity of duck. Place one onion, quartered, and one crushed garlic clove into each duck and truss.

Place the duck wings in a shallow roasting pan and place the ducks on the wings. Roast for 20 minutes in the preheated oven.

Lower temperature to 350 degrees and cook another 1½ hours, basting with drippings. Raise temperature to 475 degrees for about 15 minutes to crisp skin. Remove each duck from the pan with a long fork or spoon and drain fat from the cavity. Let cool. Split the ducks in half and remove all of the bones.

Place the ducks in the shallow pan with the stock or red wine and place back in the 475-degree oven for about 5 minutes to reheat. Place on warm plates with the Apple Shallot Mincemeat to the side and top with Marchand de Vin Sauce. *Serves 6.*

ROAST GOOSE WITH GRAVY, RED CABBAGE, AND DUMPLINGS

1 goose, approximately 10 lb. (thaw completely if frozen)	Mirepoix (1 onion, 1 carrot, and 1 celery stalk, coarsely chopped)
Salt	
Black pepper	4 tbsp. unsalted butter
2 sprigs of fresh rosemary (1 tsp. dried can be substituted)	¼ cup flour
	½ cup heavy cream
2 small firm apples, cored and peeled	Juice of ½ lemon
	Red Cabbage
1 small onion, peeled	Dumplings
½ cup water	Rosemary sprigs for garnish

Preheat the oven to 400 degrees.

Season the inside of the goose with salt and pepper. Break up the rosemary and place it in the cavity with the cored, peeled apples and whole onion. Truss the legs together with kitchen twine. Chop the neck and giblets and place them in the bottom of a roasting pan. Add ½ cup water. Set the goose, breast-side up, in the pan. Salt and pepper the outside. Roast in the preheated oven until brown, about 15 minutes or so.

Reduce the heat to 350 degrees and cook for about 3 hours, to an internal temperature of 180 degrees. Baste the goose with the pan drippings frequently. After 2 hours cover the breast with foil and place the mirepoix around the goose.

When roasted, remove the goose from the roasting pan and cut up into serving pieces. Remove the wing tips, backbone, and rib cage. Cut breast into two pieces per side and each leg and thigh piece into two pieces, eight pieces in all. When serving, two plates will have a drumstick with a boneless breast piece, the other two will have a thigh with the wing breast piece. Reserve the apples and onions for the presentation, but slice the onion.

To make the gravy, melt the butter in a medium skillet. Sprinkle in the flour and whisk constantly over moderately low heat until the mixture becomes a rich brown. Add the roasting juices and mirepoix. Simmer for 15 minutes and strain. Add the cream and lemon juice. Keep warm until service.

Arrange the goose pieces on four dinner plates. Ladle the gravy over the goose and serve with Red Cabbage and Dumplings. Garnish with the roasted apples and onion and additional fresh rosemary. *Serves 4.*

Meats

VEAL HELDER

½ medium onion, chopped
½ cup dry white wine
½ cup water
½ tsp. salt
¼ tsp. black pepper
¼ tsp. crumbled dried thyme
  leaves
6 7-oz. veal filets
Salt and pepper
2 tbsp. corn oil
4 tbsp. butter

Tomato Concasse:
1 clove crushed garlic
1 dry shallots, chopped
1 green onion, chopped, white
  only
¼ cup white wine
½ cup chopped, skinned,
  seeded tomato
Salt
White pepper
1½ cups Béarnaise Sauce

First prepare a deglazing liquid for the veal pan by combining the onion, white wine, water, salt, black pepper, and thyme in a small saucepan. Bring to a boil and reduce the liquids by half. Strain and reserve the liquids; discard the onion pulp. Hold aside.

Lightly season the veal filets with salt and white pepper. Sauté them in a skillet in hot oil for 4 minutes on each side until they are medium, or to your desired doneness. Remove the veal filets to a warm plate and hold in a warm oven.

Now deglaze pan with the onion liquids. Add the butter and tomato concasse ingredients. Reduce for 5 minutes. Add the white wine and season to taste with the salt and pepper.

To assemble, arrange each veal filet on a warm dinner plate. On one side of the veal ladle some of the Tomato Concasse, on the other side the Béarnaise Sauce. *Serves 6.*

VEAL STEAK WITH ASPARAGUS AND PINK PEPPERCORNS

6 6-oz. veal filets, trimmed of
   sidestrap
3 tbsp. cooking oil
2 tbsp. pink peppercorns (may
   substitute green)

6 tbsp. cooked, peeled, and
   pureed sweet red bell pepper
6 tbsp. butter
1½ dozen fresh cooked asparagus spears for garnish

In a hot skillet, brown the veal filets in oil on both sides and continue to cook until medium rare to medium. Remove from the skillet and pour off the excess oil.

Return to the heat and add the pink or green peppercorns and sweet red bell pepper puree while mixing and heating thoroughly. Remove from the heat and swirl in the butter until completely emulsified.

Transfer the filets to servings plates and arrange 3 asparagus spears neatly atop each. Ladle the sauce over each serving. *Serves 6.*

VEAL FARCI VERSAILLES

18 silver-dollar-size medallions
   of milk-fed veal
Salt to taste
White pepper to taste
Lemon juice to taste
1 cup all-purpose flour

4-5 beaten eggs
½ cup clarified butter
3 cups hot Crawfish Versailles
1 cup hot Brown Sauce #2
2 tbsp. chopped parsley

Season the medallions with salt, white pepper, and lemon juice. Dredge in the flour, shaking off any excess. Immerse in the beaten eggs and then put directly into the sauté pan with the hot clarified butter. Sauté until golden on each side.

For each serving put one veal medallion on a plate, cover with ½ cup heated Crawfish Versailles, then put two more medallions over this. Ladle a little of the Brown Sauce #2 over the unsauced medallions and sprinkle with fresh chopped parsley. Serve. *Serves 6.*

VEAL FILETS WITH SWEETBREADS FINANCIERE SAUCE

6 4-5 oz. veal filets
Salt
White pepper
Flour
2 tbsp. corn oil

2 cups hot Financière Sauce
18 hot Veal Quenelles
6 slices Sweetbreads
    Grenobloise

Lightly salt and pepper the veal filets and dredge in the flour. Saute briefly in hot oil until cooked to medium. Hold aside warm.

To assemble the dish, place a veal filet on each hot dinner plate. Top with a slice of the sauteed Sweetbread Grenobloise. Combine the Financière Sauce and the Veal Quenelles and spoon the mixture over the veal filets. *Serves 6.*

VEAL MEDALLIONS AND LOUISIANA CRABCAKES WITH SHITAKE-CABERNET SAUCE

12 silver-dollar-size medallions
    of milk-fed veal
Salt
White pepper
Lemon juice
¾ cup all-purpose flour
3 beaten eggs
6 tbsp. clarified butter

2 tbsp. chopped parsley
Hot crabcakes (from Louisiana
    Crabcakes with Creole Mus-
    tard-Caper Sauce)
About 2 cups Shitake-Cabernet
    Sauce
2 tbsp. chopped parsley

Season the veal medallions with the salt, pepper, and lemon juice. Dredge in the flour, shaking off any excess. Immerse in the beaten eggs and then put directly into the sauté pan with the hot clarified butter. Sauté until golden on each side.

For each serving put two veal medallions on each plate, top with a crabcake, and spoon the Shitake-Cabernet Sauce on the side. Sprinkle with chopped parsley. *Serves 6.*

VEAL FILETS STUFFED WITH SCALLOP MOUSSE

PANADA

6 tbsp. (⅜ cup) water	Pinch salt
1¼ tbsp. butter	½ cup flour

Combine the water, butter, and salt in a saucepan. Bring to a boil and add flour all at once. Mix well with a wooden spoon and cook briefly until the mixture all comes together in a boil. Transfer to a buttered plate, spread out, and chill thoroughly.

SCALLOP MOUSSE

½ lb. sea scallops	Panada
¼ tsp. salt	¼ lb. fresh butter
Pinch white pepper	1 egg
Pinch nutmeg	2 egg yolks

In a food processor grind the scallops with the salt, pepper, and nutmeg and remove. Now mix the panada and butter in the processor, add the ground scallops, and mix well. Add egg and yolks, mix well, remove, and chill.

VEAL FILETS

6 6-oz. veal tenderloins, about 4-4½ inches long	Scallop Mousse
	3 tbsp. cooking oil
6 tbsp. Dijon mustard	1 cup white wine
Salt and white pepper to taste	2 cups Brown Sauce #2
½ tbsp. fresh thyme leaves	2 tsp. lemon juice

Split the veal tenderloins open lengthwise, but don't cut all the way through. Flatten them out with a cleaver or mallet. Spread the mustard on the veal, season with the salt and pepper, and sprinkle with the thyme leaves. Spread the mousse over the meat, roll them up, and tie closed with cotton string.

Heat the oil in a saucepan or skillet and brown the veal rolls on all sides. Pour off the excess oil.

With the veal rolls in the pan, add the white wine and Brown Sauce. Simmer the rolls for about 20 minutes, or until tender. Transfer the veal rolls to serving plates, remove the strings, and sauce with the pan liquids. *Serves 6.*

PANEED VEAL ACADIAN

6 4-oz. pieces veal round
Salt and pepper to taste
1 cup white flour
Eggwash, from 2 large eggs,
beaten with 4 tbsp. heavy cream
2 cups bread crumbs
¾ cup vegetable oil

Pound out each veal piece to half of its thickness. Sprinkle with salt and pepper. Dip first in flour, then the eggwash, and then in the bread crumbs; set aside. In a heavy skillet, heat the oil. Sauté the veal until golden brown. Drain on paper towels and keep warm.

TOPPING

1 tbsp. butter
2 tsp. minced shallots
1 tbsp. fresh dill
¾ lb. jumbo lump crabmeat
Salt and pepper to taste
2¼ cups heavy cream

Melt the butter in a heavy skillet. Sauté the shallots and dill for about 2 minutes. Add the crabmeat, salt, and pepper and toss gently. Add the cream and simmer 2-3 minutes or until sauce thickens. Correct seasoning if necessary. Spoon over veal and serve. *Serves 6.*

VEAL BROUSSARD

6 6-oz. center-cut veal loin steaks
Salt and fresh ground black
   pepper
½ cup Creole mustard

½ cup butter
6 tbsp. red wine
10 tbsp. Demi-glace Sauce #2
¾ cup Tarragon Sauce

Preheat the oven to 400 degrees.

Trim veal and cut each into two 3-oz. pieces. Salt and pepper and coat with Creole mustard. In a large, heavy skillet, melt the butter. Sear veal on both sides. Deglaze the pan with the red wine and add the Demi-glace Sauce #2. Bring to a boil. Place uncovered pan in the preheated oven for 5-8 minutes. Place 2 pieces of veal on each of 6 warm plates and cover with the Tarragon Sauce. *Serves 6.*

VEAL BONAPARTE

12 2-oz. veal round slices
Salt and freshly ground black
   pepper to taste
1 cup flour
½ cup butter
Eggwash, made from 4 whole
   eggs and ½ cup water

1 lb. wild mushrooms, sliced
4 tbsp. dry red wine
½ cup Demi-glace Sauce #2 or
   Brown Sauce #2
¾ cup Creole Mustard-Caper
   Sauce

Pound out veal to half of its thickness. Sprinkle with salt and pepper and dust with flour. In a heavy skillet melt 6 tablespoons of the butter. Dip floured veal in the eggwash and sauté. Keep warm.

In another pan melt the remaining 2 tablespoons of butter and sauté mushrooms. Deglaze the pan with the red wine and reduce by half. Add Demi-glace or Brown Sauce and simmer until thick.

Place one slice of veal on each of 6 warm plates and top with mushrooms. Place second veal slice on top and cover with 4 tablespoons of Creole Mustard-Caper Sauce. *Serves 6.*

VEAL SCALLOPINI "MICADO"

8 3-oz. pieces Veal Scallopini
½ cup carrots, julienned
½ cup celery, julienned
½ cup leeks, julienned
½ cup onions, diced
2 cloves garlic, minced

½ cup walnut or olive oil
1 tbsp. lemon juice
½ cup water
Salt and black pepper to taste
¼ cup parsley, chopped

Preheat the oven to 350 degrees.

Sear veal on each side in a sauté pan. Transfer the veal to a plate.

To the same pan add the carrots, celery, leeks, onions, garlic, walnut or olive oil, lemon juice, and water. Place the veal on top of the vegetables and cover the pan with foil. Bake in the preheated oven for 10 minutes. Season to taste with salt and pepper. Serve 2 pieces of veal per portion with the pan vegetables and juices. Garnish with parsley. *Serves 4.*

VEAL FLORENTINE

6 veal top round steaks
½ lb. fresh spinach, stems
  removed and chopped
½ lb. fresh chopped mushrooms
2 oz. smoked ham, minced
2 tbsp. chopped garlic
½ cup cream
Salt and white pepper to taste
½ cup or more French bread
  crumbs

1 cup flour
3 eggs, beaten
3 tbsp. butter
3 cups Tomato Sauce
3 cups Brown Sauce #2
2 tbsp. butter
1 large tomato, peeled, seeded,
  and cut into small julienne
  strips

"Pocket" the veal steaks by cutting an incision into the side of the steak and opening up a "pocket" to hold the seasoning ingredients. Combine the spinach, mushrooms, ham, garlic, and cream in a saucepan. Bring to a boil and cook 3-4 minutes. Season to taste with salt and pepper. Stir in enough bread crumbs to attain a stuffing-type consistency. Allow to cool.

Stuff each veal steak with the mixture and press on open pocket edges to seal. Sprinkle with salt and pepper, coat with flour, then dip in the beaten egg. Sauté on each side in the butter in a skillet until golden brown. Make a sauce with 2 parts Tomato Sauce and 1 part Brown Sauce, finishing with fresh butter.

Top each steak with the julienned tomato, cover with sauce, and serve. *Serves 6.*

FRICASSEE OF VEAL WITH CAPERS AND DILL

4 lb. veal cutlets, cut into 1-inch strips.
Water to cover
Salt
2 cups white wine
1 onion, sliced
3 bay leaves
5 whole cloves
½ cup butter
¾ cup flour
1 tbsp. capers
1 tsp. chopped dill
White pepper to taste
Pinch nutmeg
1 cup heavy cream
2 egg yolks
6 cups cooked rice or noodles

Place the veal strips in a saucepan and evenly cover with water. Bring to a slow boil, then rinse clean. Cover the veal again with water. Season with the salt, add the white wine, onion, bay leaves, and cloves. Simmer until cooked. Strain and reserve liquids.

Make a white roux with the butter and flour. Whisk in the strained cooking liquor and bring to a simmer. Add the capers, dill, white pepper, and nutmeg. Adjust seasonings to taste, add the cooked veal to the sauce, and simmer 10 more minutes.

Before serving, mix the heavy cream and egg yolks and pour very slowly in the fricasse. Allow the liquids to warm without coming to a boil. Serve with the rice or noodles. *Serves 8.*

VEAL QUENELLES

½ lb. ground lean veal
3 egg whites
2 tbsp. brandy

2 tsp. chopped parsley
½ tsp. salt or to taste
¼ tsp. white pepper or to taste

POACHING LIQUID

2 pints water
¼ cup white wine

1 clove-studded onion

Combine the ground veal in a blender container with the egg whites, brandy, parsley, salt, and white pepper. Process until smooth.

In a saucepan or sauté pan, combine the water, white wine, and clove-studded onion. Bring to a boil and boil for 2 minutes.

To cook the quenelles, use a wet teaspoon to form little dumplings from the meat mixture. Slide them into the poaching liquid and cook until done, about 3 minutes. Do this in batches so as not to crowd the pan. Use immediately or store covered in the refrigerator until ready for use. *Makes 18 small dumplings.*

Serve with sweetbread, veal, and game dishes.

WIENER SCHNITZEL

6 4-oz. slices of veal top round
Salt
White pepper
2 tbsp. lemon juice
1 cup flour
3 eggs, beaten
1 cup bread crumbs

4 tbsp. margarine
6 tbsp. butter
2 peeled lemons, sliced very
  thin and seeded
6 rolled anchovy filets with
  capers

Pound the veal round slices very thin. Season them with the salt and white pepper and sprinkle them with the lemon juice. Dredge the veal pieces in the flour, dip in the beaten eggs, and dredge in the bread crumbs.

Heat the margarine in a wide skillet and sauté the veal pieces on both sides until golden brown. Arrange on warm dinner plates.

Put the butter in a clean sauté pan and heat until brown. Pour over the schnitzel and garnish with the peeled lemon slices and a rolled anchovy filet with capers. *Serves 6.*

SAUTEED CALF'S LIVER

12 slices bacon	½ cup flour
2½ lb. calf's liver, cut into 12 thin slices	2 tbsp. butter
	Juice from 1 lemon
1 tsp. salt	1 tbsp. chopped parsley

In a skillet, sauté the slices of bacon. Cook the bacon until it is crisp, drain it on paper towels, and set it aside to keep hot.

Season the thin slices of calf's liver with a little salt and sprinkle them with flour. Brown them quickly on both sides in the hot bacon fat. Arrange the liver on a serving dish and keep it warm.

Discard the fat from the pan in which the liver was cooked but do not wash the pan. Add the butter to the pan and cook it until it is brown. Sprinkle the liver with a few drops of lemon juice, pour the browned butter over it, and sprinkle it with chopped parsley. Garnish the platter with the crisp bacon. *Serves 6, allowing 2 slices each.*

MARINATED PORK TENDERLOIN WITH APPLES, CELERY, AND LOUISIANA SWEET POTATO HASHBROWNS

MARINADE

6 tbsp. sliced carrots	½ cup salad oil
4 tbsp. sliced onions	4 cloves bruised garlic
2 tbsp. sliced celery	5 sprigs fresh thyme (½ tsp. dry)
1 cup soy sauce	6 6-oz. pork tenderloin filets
⅔ cup white wine	

In a bowl, combine all of the marinade ingredients. Now place the pork filets and the marinade in a pan just large enough to hold all snugly. Cover and refrigerate for at least 24 hours. Turn the pork filets several times during the marinating period.

SAUCE

3 oz. (6 tbsp.) oil or clarified margarine for cooking
1 cup white wine
1½ tbsp. Dijon-style mustard
1 tsp. chopped shallots
2 tbsp. fresh butter
1 tsp. chopped garlic
1 cup Brown Sauce #2
1 tsp. white vinegar
Dash hot pepper sauce
Salt to taste
White pepper to taste
2 tbsp. butter
Sauteed Apples
Sauteed Celery Julienne
Louisiana Sweet Potato Hash Browns
6 sprigs fresh thyme for garnish

Preheat the oven to 400 degrees.

Heat a covered skillet or dutch oven very hot. Add the oil or clarified margarine and then place the filets in carefully and brown well on both sides. Remove the filets to a plate and pour off the excess margarine from skillet. Add the white wine, mustard, shallots, butter, and garlic to the skillet. Mix well to dissolve the mustard. Add the Brown Sauce #2, vinegar, and hot pepper sauce and mix well. Return the pork filets to the sauce along with any juice they've accumulated. Place in the preheated oven for 8-10 minutes until medium-cooked. Remove filets from skillet and keep warm. Return skillet to stovetop to heat. Add the fresh butter to the skillet. Season to taste with salt and pepper.

Serve the dish on heated plates. Place the Sauteed Celery in the upper right quarter, toward the middle. Lay the apple wedges in a shingled fashion in the upper left quarter next to the celery. Place a hash brown potato leaning on the celery at the right side of the plate. Slice pork filets from top to bottom on a bias into four even slices. "Fan out" slices of pork on the left side of plate, resting two first slices on apple wedges. Spoon sauce onto left side of plate over the pork and garnish with a sprig or two of fresh thyme. *Serves 6.*

SMOKED PORK LOIN

2 lb. rock salt
1 lb. brown sugar
10 crushed bay leaves
2 tsp. chopped garlic
4 medium chopped onions
2 tsp. cracked peppercorns

2 bunches parsley, chopped
1 4½-lb. boneless pork loin
1 cup white wine
2 cups Demi-glace Sauce #1
Sauerkraut

Combine the rock salt, brown sugar, bay leaves, garlic, onions, peppercorns, and parsley. Place pork loin in this mixture and allow to cure for 3-4 days. Remove and rinse. Smoke in a home smoker for 40 minutes. After smoking, cut the loin into chops and grill, or roast whole in a 350-degree oven, until done (consider the 40-minute smoking time when cooking).

Deglaze the pan with the white wine and add the Demi-glace Sauce. Season carefully with salt and pepper if desired. Slice and serve with Sauerkraut. *Serves 6.*

Note: This dish can be prepared without the smoking. Simply cook the pork longer.

BRAISED LOIN OF PORK BOULANGERE

1 4½-lb. loin of pork, seasoned
   with 1 tsp. salt
1 cup stock or water
2 tbsp. buerre manie (1 tbsp.
   softened butter blended with
   1 tbsp. flour)
8 potatoes, peeled and sliced

½ cup chopped onions
1 tbsp. chopped parsley
1 tsp. salt
Pinch black pepper
2 tbsp. melted butter
1 cup hot water

Preheat the oven to 375 degrees.

Put the pork loin in a deep roasting pan. Roast the meat in the preheated oven for 1½ hours, or until brown, turning it several times. Remove the pork from the pan; pour off the fat.

Make a pan gravy with stock or water and stir to dissolve all the browned juices in the pan. Thicken the gravy with the beurre manie and pour it out of the pan. Hold aside.

Mix the potatoes with the onions, parsley, salt, and pepper. Spread the seasoned potatoes in the roasting pan and sprinkle them with the melted butter. Put the meat on top and spread it with 2 tablespoons of the gravy. Add the hot water, enough to come to the top of the potatoes. Cover the pan, bring the liquid to a boil, and braise in a moderate oven, 350 degrees, for about 1½ hours, or until the bones separate easily from the meat and the potatoes are golden brown. Reheat the gravy and serve with the meat and potatoes. *Serves 8-10.*

BEEF MOELLE

½ cup red wine
2 tbsp. dry shallots, chopped
Pinch black pepper
½ bay leaf
Sprig of thyme
1½ cups Brown Sauce
1 cup fresh mushrooms, sliced

6 6-8 oz. filet mignons
Salt and black pepper to taste
Corn oil
Toast rounds
½ lb. beef marrow, chilled and
    sliced, from butcher

Combine the red wine, shallots, black pepper, bay leaf, and thyme in a saucepan. Reduce by half. Add the Brown Sauce and mushrooms. Mix well and reduce to the desired thickness. Hold aside warm.

Salt and pepper the steaks, drizzle with the oil and grill or broil to desired doneness. Place the cooked filets on toast rounds, top each filet with a few slices of bone marrow, and pass through an oven to heat and gently melt the marrow. Surround with the mushroom sauce and serve. *Serves 6.*

SLICED BEEF STEW

1 2½-lb. rump roast
2 tbsp. beef or veal fat
2 tbsp. vinegar
1 cup beer
3 cups beef stock
1 tsp. sugar
3 large onions, chopped
2 tbsp. butter
2 tbsp. flour

Bouquet Garni (wrap in cheese-
    cloth and tie together with
    cotton string):
1 stalk celery
3 sprigs parsley
1 bay leaf
Sprig thyme
4 tbsp. tomato sauce (optional)

Preheat the oven to 325 degrees.

Cut the roast into twelve slices and flatten each with a mallet. Heat the fat in a skillet and sauté the meat on both sides, a few pieces at a time. Remove them to a plate as they are browned. When all have been cooked, pour off the fat in the pan, add the vinegar, and stir in all the brown crustiness in the pan. Add the beer, the beef stock, and sugar and simmer for a few minutes.

In another pan, sauté the chopped the onions in the butter until they are golden and soft. Stir in the flour and cook together until the flour begins to brown.

Put a layer of the sauteed onions in a casserole and add some of the sauce from the skillet and a layer of the browned meat slices. Continue to add onions, sauce, and meat until all ingredients are used. Add the bouquet garni. Tomato sauce may be added.

Strain the remaining sauce over all and add any juice that is left on the plate that held the browned meat. There should be just enough liquid to cover the contents. If not, add a little hot water.

Cover the casserole with a lid that has a small hole in it, or just barely askew. Bring to a boil and cook in the preheated oven for 2-2½ hours. Serve from the casserole. *Serves 4-5.*

GRILLED PETIT FILET MIGNON WITH BEARNAISE AND PORT WINE SAUCES

6 6-8 oz. beef filets
Salt
Black pepper to taste

Béarnaise Sauce
Port Sauce

Season the beef filets with salt and black pepper and grill to your preferred doneness.

To serve the Petit Filet Mignon, place each on a hot dinner plate and ladle Béarnaise Sauce over one-half of the steak and Port Sauce over the other. These two sauces served together deliver a good taste contrast as well as an effective color contrast. *Serves 6.*

FILET JOSEPHINE

6 8-oz. filets of beef
Salt and freshly ground black
  pepper

1½ cups Port Sauce
¾ cup Béarnaise Sauce

Preheat the grill or broiler. If using broiler, also preheat broiling pan.

Sprinkle filets with salt and pepper. If using broiler, brush pan with butter or vegetable oil before you place the filets on. Cook until desired degree of doneness. Place on warm plates.

Serve with 4 tablespoons of Port Wine Sauce over each filet and 2 tablespoons of Béarnaise Sauce in the center of each filet. *Serves 6.*

BEEF ROULADEN

1 medium onion, chopped
1 tbsp. butter
6 4-oz. slices of beef top round
Salt to taste
Black pepper to taste
Dijon mustard to taste
1 large dill pickle

6 slices bacon
6 toothpicks
Hot oil
Brown Sauce #1
Red Cabbage
Dumplings

Sauté the onion in the butter until limp; cool in refrigerator.

Have your butcher flatten the beef slices, or pound them yourself. Preheat the oven to 350 degrees.

Lay the flattened beef slices on the counter, season with the salt and pepper and spread with Dijon mustard. Cut pickle into six spears. Add a slice of raw bacon, a pickle spear, and some chopped onions to each beef roll. Roll the meat up around the ingredients and put a toothpick through to hold during cooking.

Put these "rouladen" in hot oil and braise in the preheated oven. Pour off the excess grease and add the Brown Sauce #1. Cook beef rolls for one hour or until done. Remove the toothpicks and place cooked rolls on warm plates. Serve the beef rolls with Red Cabbage and Dumplings. *Serves 6.*

BEEF TENDERLOIN STUFFED WITH VEAL TENDERLOIN

2 6-oz. veal filets, flattened
  with a mallet
Salt and pepper to taste
¼ cup Dijon mustard
1½ lb. beef tenderloin, strap
  removed, well trimmed, flattened a with mallet
½ tsp. dried thyme
½ tsp. chopped garlic

3 tbsp. cooking oil
1 cup white wine
2 tbsp. chopped shallots
¼ tsp. thyme
½ bay leaf
2 cups Brown Sauce #2
1 tbsp. fresh tarragon
1 tbsp. fresh butter

Preheat the oven to 450 degrees.

Season veal filet pieces with salt, pepper, and Dijon mustard and sear in a very hot pan on one side (the outside) until just browned, keeping veal as rare as possible. Cool.

Lay beef tenderloin out flat with cut-side up. Rub with the Dijon mustard and garlic; sprinkle with thyme, salt, and pepper. Lay veal tenderloin's browned side down onto the center of the beef, ends can overlap slightly. Fold over two long sides of beef to the middle, keeping veal tenderloins intact on the inside. Carefully turn beef over with "seam" side down. Using butcher's twine, loop string around beef at 1-inch to 2-inch intervals to hold the whole thing together. Secure string well in order to keep beef/veal from falling apart during cooking and handling.

Season beef with salt, pepper, and mustard and brown quickly in the cooking oil in a hot, ovenproof skillet. Remove the beef and deglaze the skillet with the white wine, add the shallots, thyme, and bay leaf and reduce by half. Add the brown sauce, mix well, and bring to a simmer.

Return beef to the sauce with any juices, then cook in the preheated oven for 20-25 minutes, basting with sauce several times. Remove bay leaf from sauce. Return sauce to heat on the stovetop and reduce to desired consistency. Add fresh tarragon leaves and finish with the fresh butter.

Cut the string from beef/veal with scissors, slice carefully, and place on warmed plates, surround with the sauce, and serve. *Serves 6.*

POT AU FEU

2 qt. water
Salt to taste
Black pepper to taste
2 cups rough-chopped greens
   from leeks
1 cup parsley stems
2 medium onions, halved
2 bay leaves
4 lb. lean brisket

1 small cabbage
3 carrots
¼ bunch parsley
1 celery root or 3 pieces celery
2 leeks, white part only
12 ½-inch marrow bones
Chopped parsley for garnish
Garlic toasts from French bread

Simmer meat for 1½ hours in the water, skimming regularly until three-fourths done. Season to taste with salt and pepper. To create stock for soup add salt, pepper, greens from leeks, parsley stems, onions, and bay leaves.

Brown brisket and add to stock. (Other options are shortribs, beef shoulder, or lean stew meat.)

Cut caggage, carrots, leeks (white part) into 1-inch pieces. Wash and layer in heavy pot. Strain beef broth on top, put brisket on vegetables and simmer until vegetables and meat are done.

Five minutes before serving, blanch the marrow bones. Do not loose marrow from bones. Slice beef and serve in soup bowl on top of vegetables. Garnish with marrow bones, chopped parsley, and garlic toast. *Serves 6.*

SIRLOIN OF BEEF MADAGASCAR

1 cup Dijon mustard
½ cup brandy
3 tbsp. fresh cracked black pepper
6 14-oz. sirloin steaks
1 tbsp. butter

1 tbsp. minced shallots
4 tbsp. brandy
2 cups heavy cream
1 small round Boursin cheese
Salt and white pepper to taste

Mix the Dijon mustard, brandy, and black pepper. Coat the sirloins with this mixture and wrap in plastic film and refrigerate overnight.

In a heavy saucepan, melt butter and sauté the shallots until soft.

Deglaze the pan with 4 tablespoons of brandy and reduce by half. Add the cream and bring to a boil. Reduce and simmer for about 5 minutes or until the cream thickens. Remove from heat and mix in the cheese in small pieces. Check seasoning and adjust if necessary. Keep warm.

Place sirloins on a preheated broiling pan or grill and cook to desired doneness. Transfer to heated plates and top with about 4 tablespoons of sauce. *Serves 6.*

RACK OF LAMB AUX HERBES

3 20-oz. lamb racks
2 tbsp. butter
3 cups plain bread crumbs
2 tsp. fresh rosemary, chopped fine
½ tsp. dried thyme leaves

2 tsp. minced garlic
1 tsp. fresh cracked black pepper
½ cup extra virgin olive oil
¾ cup Dijon mustard
1½ cups Rosemary-Mint Fond

Have your butcher French-trim the lamb racks.

Preheat the oven to 375 degrees.

Cut the racks in half so you have 6 small racks with equal chops. In a heavy skillet, melt the butter and sear racks on all sides until brown. Set aside to cool.

In a large bowl, combine the bread crumbs, rosemary, thyme, garlic, pepper, and olive oil and mix well. Spread the mustard on all sides of the cooled racks and press the bread-crumb mixture into the mustard. Place on heated rack or pan in the preheated oven and cook for about 15-20 minutes. Place on heated plates and top with Rosemary-Mint Fond. *Serves 6.*

LAMB FLORENTINE

6 boneless lamb racks or loins,
    trimmed, seasoned with salt
    and pepper, and rubbed with
    Dijon mustard
3 cups Florentine Spinach
6 5-by-7-inch puff pastry sheets
4 egg yolks

Nonstick vegetable spray
1 cup red Burgundy wine
2 tbsp. mint jelly
1 sprig fresh rosemary
2 cups Brown Sauce #2
1 tbsp. fresh butter

Preheat the oven to 375-400 degrees.

In a very hot skillet, sear the lamb until browned on the outside, keeping it as rare as possible. Chill.

Lay some Florentine Spinach in the center of each puff pastry rectangle the length of the lamb pieces. Lay a lamb piece on each portion of spinach, then top each lamb with the remaining spinach mixture.

Trim a small square from each of the four corners of the puff pastry (to avoid excess pastry) then rub all four edges of the pasty with egg yolk. Now fold the two longer sides to the middle and overlap them, allowing the egg yolk to act as an adhesive. Seal the two ends in the same fashion.

Flip each lamb/pastry over and place on a baking sheet previously sprayed with the vegetable spray. Use remaining egg yolks and coat the tops and sides of each pastry, not liberally but thoroughly.

Bake in the preheated degree oven about 15-20 minutes, or until puffed and golden brown.

Meanwhile, in a skillet combine the Burgundy, mint jelly, and rosemary and reduce by half. Add Brown Sauce and reduce again by half. Taste for salt and pepper, remove rosemary, and finish with fresh butter.

Carefully remove lamb pastries from the oven, cut in half on a diagonal from top to bottom and place on warmed plates, angling each half to expose spinach and medium-rare lamb. Surround with sauce and serve. *Serves 6.*

SIRLOIN OR LOIN OF VENISON BLACK FOREST-STYLE WITH TARRAGON SAUCE

2 sirloins or loins of venison, well aged
3-4 strips bacon (optional)
4-5 strips Westphalian ham (or prosciutto)
1½ cups dry red wine
Juice from 3 lemons
1 tsp. grated lemon rind
2 onions, thinly sliced
4 sprigs tarragon
10 peppercorns, crushed
5 juniper berries, crushed
5 cloves, crushed
4 bay leaves, crumbled
1 medium carrot, scraped and sliced thin
1 parsnip, scraped and sliced thin
4 strips bacon, minced
1½ cups Riesling wine
Salt
Coarsely ground black pepper
Venison Tarragon Sauce

If desired, venison filets may be larded. Insert thin strips bacon and Westphalian ham into larding needle and pass needle through meat.

Place filets in a shallow dish. Add the dry red wine, lemon juice, lemon rind, 1 of the sliced onions, tarragon, peppercorns, juniper berries, cloves, and bay leaves. Turn meat several times. Cover the dish and refrigerate for 10-12 hours, turning meat several times.

Preheat the oven to 350 degrees. Remove the filets and pat dry with paper towels. Strain the marinade and reserve. Also reserve the onion and seasonings from marinade. Spread the second onion, carrots, and parsnip in the bottom of a roasting pan. Sprinkle vegetables with minced bacon. Add Riesling wine and reserved onions and seasonings from marinade. Sprinkle filets with salt and coarsely ground black pepper. Place meat in roasting pan and roast in the preheated oven—17 minutes per pound for rare, 20-22 minutes for medium rare, 24-26 minutes for well done. Baste often with pan juices. Serve thinly sliced with the following sauce made with the pan drippings.

VENISON TARRAGON SAUCE

4 tbsp. unsalted butter	Salt
1½ cups Riesling wine	Pepper
5 shallots, minced	Juice from one lemon
Reserved strained marinade	1 tsp. grated lemon rind
Strained pan juices	1-2 tbsp. brown sugar to taste
1 tsp. tarragon, minced	

In saucepan, combine butter, 1 cup of the Riesling wine, and shallots and cook until mixture has been reduced by a third and is slightly thickened. Add the reserved strained marinade and strained pan juices. Simmer 5 minutes. Add remaining ingredients and the remaining ½ cup of wine. Cook over moderate heat until reduced by about a third or slightly thickened. Adjust seasoning and serve over the sliced venison or on the side. *Serves 6-8.*

WILD BOAR GRILL

3 qt. buttermilk	1 tbsp. minced garlic
5 medium yellow onions, sliced	1 tbsp. juniper berries, crushed
4 green onions, sliced	½ cup white wine
2 medium carrots, sliced	6 8-oz. wild boar chops
2 celery ribs, sliced	Salt
½ cup chopped parsley	Black pepper
¼ cup black peppercorns	1¾ cups Red Currant Sauce

In a stainless steel or glass bowl, combine the buttermilk with the yellow onions, green onions, carrots, celery, and chopped parsley. Stir in the black peppercorns, garlic, juniper berries, and white wine. Cover the bowl and refrigerate overnight to give this marinade time for the seasoning ingredients to release their flavors into the buttermilk.

To marinate the boar chops, trim off any excess fat and lay them into the marinade, stirring all the ingredients around so that all the chops are completely covered by the marinade. Cover the bowl, place it in the refrigerator, and marinate for 1-2 days, depending on the "wildness" of the game's flavor.

To cook the chops, remove them from the marinade, allow the vegetables and liquids to drip off, then season the chops with salt and pepper. Place the chops on a grill or under a broiler and cook to medium or your desired doneness. Turn once during the cooking. Serve the Grilled Wild Boar Chops with Red Currant Sauce. *Serves 6.*

Any wild game or fowl can be used in this preparation.

WILD BOAR WITH POTATO STRUDEL AND CARAMELIZED APPLES AND ONIONS

WILD BOAR

10 oz. smoked bacon, diced	½ cup skinned diced celery
3 lb. wild boar leg, boned, trimmed of fat and gristle, and cut into 1-inch cubes	1½ tbsp. Dijon mustard
	1½ tbsp. red currant jelly
	1½ tbsp. juniper berries, crushed
Salt	
Black pepper	1½ cups red wine
4 onions, diced	6 oz. chicken livers, pureed
3 carrots, diced	2 cups Demi-glace Sauce #1

Sauté the diced smoked bacon and the boar cubes in a large pan until the cubes are browned. Season with salt and black pepper and add the onions, carrots, celery, mustard, red currant jelly, and juniper berries. Stir all together with the red wine and simmer gently for an hour. Remove the boar cubes, strain the pan ingredients, reserving both liquids and solids, and thicken the strained solids with the pureed livers and Demi-glace Sauce to make a ragout. Hold aside.

POTATO STRUDEL

3 cups flour
¾ cup warm water
1½ tbsp. vegetable oil
Pinch salt to taste
3 lb. potatoes, boiled and
 skinned
1 large egg

1¼ lb. finely diced steamed
 vegetables ("brunoise"—carrots, celery, onions)
½ cup chopped parsley
Black pepper to taste
Nutmeg to taste
½ cup melted butter

Make the strudel dough by combining then kneading the flour, water, oil and a pinch of salt, and allow to stand for 30 minutes. Preheat the oven to 400 degrees.

Boil the potatoes in salted water. Mash them. Add the egg, vegetable brunoise, parsley, black pepper, and nutmeg and work to a smooth paste. Roll out the strudel dough, place on a damp towel, and spread with a layer of the potato paste. Dribble with melted butter. Roll the mixture into strudel form, brush with butter, and bake in the preheated oven for 30 minutes.

CARAMELIZED APPLES AND ONIONS

3 apples
1¼ lb. pearl onions, skinned
¾ cup butter

¾ cup sugar
¾ cup red wine

Core and peel the apples and slice them into eight wedges each. Sauté the onions with the apples in the butter, sprinkle with sugar, add the red wine, and simmer until tender. To serve, place diagonally cut wedges of the strudel with the wild boar on a warm plate. Decorate with the caramelized apples and onions, and spoon the sauce over. *Serves 6.*

This is an excellent preparation for leg of venison, elk, or buffalo.

SWEETBREADS GRENOBLOISE

3 lb. fresh or frozen sweetbreads
Water
½ cup white wine
1 onion, peeled
10 cloves
2 bay leaves

Salt
White pepper
2 tbsp. lemon juice
1 cup flour
¼ lb. butter
1⅓ cups Grenobloise Sauce

Rinse and wash the sweetbreads and remove any gristle or fat. Place the sweetbreads in a pot and cover with water. Bring the water to a boil to blanch the sweetbreads then rinse them under cold water. Again cover the sweetbreads in the pot with fresh water, add the white wine, a peeled onion studded with several whole cloves, and the bay leaves. Bring to a gentle simmer and cook for 30-40 minutes, or until done. Refrigerate in the cooking liquids.

When finishing, slice cold into three slices per portion. Season with salt, white pepper, and a sprinkle of lemon juice. Dredge in the flour and sauté in hot butter briefly on both sides. Add the pan drippings to the Grenobloise Sauce. To serve, place three slices of sweetbreads on each of six dinner plates and top with the Grenobloise Sauce. *Serves 6.*

Desserts and Sweet Sauces

ALMOND COOKIES WITH MOCHA SAUCE AND CREAM NOISETTE

CREAM NOISETTE

¾ cup hazelnut paste
6 oz. egg yolk (yolks from about 8 eggs)
¼ cup sugar

1 tbsp. gelatin
¼ cup brandy
1 cup milk
2 cups whipped heavy cream

In a double boiler combine the hazelnut paste, egg yolks, sugar, gelatin, brandy, and milk. Whisk while heating until the mixture thickens. Chill in the refrigerator. Then fold in the whipped heavy cream and refrigerate for another hour.

ALMOND COOKIE SHELLS

¼ tbsp. butter
½ cup sugar
¼ cup egg white
⅓ cup finely chopped almonds

¼ tbsp. almond extract
¼ tsp. vanilla extract
Butter to grease the baking sheets

Cream the butter in a bowl with the sugar. Whisk in the egg whites, finely chopped almonds, and almond and vanilla extracts. Preheat the oven to 425 degrees. Butter the baking sheets. Drop table-spoon dollops of cookie batter on sheets, spacing them 3 inches apart. With the back of a spoon, flatten out each dollop into a thin, 2½-inch disk. Bake for 4 minutes. When done, carefully lift each cookie with a metal spatula. Place over a small glass dish and form into a cup. Let cool and stiffen.

TOPPINGS

Mocha Sauce
Whipped cream for garnish

Glazed cherries for garnish

To serve, place the cookie shells on glass dessert plates. Spoon some Mocha Sauce into each Almond Cookie Shell, then a scoop of Cream Noisette. Decorate with whipped cream and a glazed cherry. *Serves 6.*

BANANAS FOSTER

4 tbsp. butter
¼ cup light brown sugar
¼ cup dark brown sugar
¼ cup 151 rum
¼ cup banana liqueur

½ tsp. cinnamon
½ cup water
3 bananas, quartered
6 ½-cup scoops vanilla ice
  cream

Put butter, light brown sugar, and dark brown sugar in a pan. Melt until everything is dissolved and almost like a paste. Flame with the rum and add the banana liqueur. Add the cinnamon and water and cook until it becomes a semi-thick sauce. Cook the bananas in the sauce until almost soft.

For each serving, in a deep dish, use 1 scoop of vanilla ice cream, top with 2 pieces of banana, and serve hot. *Serves 6.*

BREAD PUDDING WITH RUM SAUCE

6 eggs
3 cups milk
1 cup canned fruit cocktail
½ cup raisins
¾ cup sugar
½ cup Meyer's dark rum

½ tbsp. vanilla extract
½ tbsp. yellow food coloring
6 8-inch loaves stale French
  bread
½ lb. melted butter
Rum Sauce

Preheat the oven to 350 degrees.

In a bowl, beat the eggs and whisk in the milk. Stir in the fruit cocktail, raisins, sugar, rum, vanilla, and food coloring. Stir until the sugar is dissolved.

Tear the bread into small pieces and add them to the bowl. Allow the bread to soak up the liquids. Fold them around a few times to distribute the fruits. Stir in the melted butter.

Spoon the mixture into a buttered deep baking pan and bake for 1 hour in the preheated oven, or until golden brown on top and the custard is set. Serve hot or cold with the Rum Sauce spooned over. *Serves 12.*

This is also good served with Mocha Sauce or Praline Sauce.

CARAMEL CUP CUSTARD

7 tbsp. sugar
¼ cup water
2 cups milk

4 eggs
7 tbsp. sugar
1 tsp. vanilla extract

Preheat the oven to 325 degrees.

Combine 7 tablespoons of sugar and water and cook until golden brown, or slightly caramelized. Coat the inside of 6 custard cups and allow to cool to room temperature.

Heat the milk to boiling. In a separate bowl, beat the eggs thoroughly, add sugar, and mix well. Stream the hot milk into the egg mixture, whisking vigorously, and add the vanilla.

Pour this custard into the caramelized cups and place in a pan of hot water. Cook in the preheated oven for about 30 minutes. Remove and refrigerate. To serve, invert the cups on individual dessert plates and allow the liquid caramel to flow down the sides and onto the plate. Garnish as desired and serve. *Serves 6.*

CHESTNUT AND CHOCOLATE TERRINE

1 lb. chestnut puree
4 oz. sweet chocolate, melted
½ cup softened butter
1 tsp. vanilla extract

1½ oz. (3 tbsp.) Frangelico
 liqueur
2 tsp. grated orange zest
Raspberry Sauce

Heat the chestnut puree in a saucepan. Add the melted chocolate, softened butter, vanilla, liqueur, and orange zest. Blend all well together. Put the mixture in a square cake pan lined with wax paper. Chill overnight. Slice and serve with Raspberry Sauce. *Serves 6.*

CHOCOLATE ESPRESSO SOUFFLE

Butter
9 oz. semisweet chocolate
  pieces, or grated
1½ cups double-strength
  espresso

6 large egg whites
Pinch salt
1 cup sugar
1 tbsp. butter

Preheat the oven to 375 degrees.

Lightly butter a 1½- to 2-quart soufflé mold, or six individual soufflé molds. Set aside.

In a double boiler, melt the semisweet chocolate and whisk in the double-strength espresso.

Make the meringue by whipping the egg whites in a bowl with a pinch of salt until they form soft peaks. Slowly add the sugar, continuing to whip the whites as you go. Whip until the sugar is dissolved.

Transfer the chocolate-espresso mixture to a bowl and fold in several tablespoonfuls of the meringue to lighten it. Fold in the remaining meringue a third at a time. Do not overwork the mixture. Spoon the soufflé mixture into the buttered soufflé mold or molds. Place the molds in a pan of hot water and the whole pan into the preheated oven. Bake for 35-40 minutes, or until the soufflé has risen and browned nicely on the top. *Serves 6.*

CHOCOLATE PAVA

4 oz. unsweetened chocolate
½ cup fresh butter
6 tbsp. sugar

5 eggs, separated
Raspberry Sauce
1½ cups freshly whipped cream

In a double boiler, gently melt the chocolate and butter with the sugar, stirring to mix until the chocolate and sugar are dissolved. Cool the mixture in refrigerator to about room temperature.

Beat the egg yolks to the ribbon stage, add to the chocolate, and mix well. Return mixture to the refrigerator. When completely cool, beat the egg whites to the stiff-peak stage and fold into the chocolate a third at a time. Refrigerate again for about 30 minutes or until Pava is set. Serve with Raspberry Sauce and freshly whipped cream. *Serves 6.*

Try this served with English Tia Maria Cream.

CHOCOLATE SALAMI

6 oz. bittersweet chocolate, pieces or grated	1²/₃ cups hot scalded heavy cream
6 oz. semisweet chocolate, pieces or grated	1 cup shelled pistachios, coarsely chopped and lightly roasted
5 tbsp. butter	Pistachio Sauce

Combine the bittersweet and semisweet chocolates with the butter in the top of a double boiler. Whisk together when the chocolate is melted into a smooth consistency.

Pour the hot scalded heavy cream into a bowl and slowly whisk in the chocolate mixture. Blend well and add the chopped pistachios. Cover the bowl with foil or plastic wrap and chill in the refrigerator. Remove the cover and whip the mixture every 15 minutes. Continue this process until the mixture is cold enough to hold its own shape.

Roll the mixture into a cylinder shape about 2¼ inches in diameter. Wrap tightly in plastic wrap and chill for several hours, or until firm. Cut into ½-inch-thick pieces using a sharp knife dipped in hot water. To serve, spoon some of the Pistachio Sauce onto each dessert plate and top with two of the chocolate rounds. *Serves 6.*

CHOCOLATE TERRINE WITH ENGLISH TIA MARIA CREAM

3½ tbsp. sugar
Water
7 oz. (14 tbsp.) walnuts
7 oz. (14 tbsp.) chocolate
1½ tbsp. peanut oil
7 tbsp. butter, softened

3 large egg yolks
3 large egg whites
Pinch salt
2 tbsp. sugar
¾ cup whipped cream
English Tia Maria Cream

Preheat the oven to 375 degrees.

Combine the sugar with a little water and add the walnuts. Stir them around until they are well coated. Place the sugared walnuts on a baking sheet and place in the preheated oven for about 5 minutes, or long enough to caramelize the sugar coating. Cool.

Combine the chocolate and peanut oil together in the top of a double boiler and heat until the chocolate is melted. Mix thoroughly.

Combine the butter and egg yolks in a bowl and beat until smooth.

In another bowl, whip the egg whites with the salt until they stand in soft peaks. Gradually beat in the 2 tablespoons of sugar a little at a time, and whip until the sugar is dissolved and the white meringue stands in stiff peaks. Whip the chocolate mixture into the egg yolk mixture. Carefully fold in the whipped cream, then the egg white meringue. Fold in the caramelized walnuts and spoon the mixture into a terrine or soufflé mold. Cover the container and hold in the freezer for 8 hours or overnight.

To serve the Chocolate Terrine, use a hot wet knife blade to separate it from the sides of the mold and unmold it onto a plate. Slice it into 12 rounds and serve 2 per person with English Tia Maria Cream spooned on the side. *Serves 6.*

CREME BRULEE

5 egg yolks
1 cup plus 6 tbsp. sugar
1 tbsp. vanilla extract

2 cups heavy cream
6 tbsp. sugar

Preheat the oven to 300 degrees.

Mix the egg yolks, sugar, and vanilla in mixing bowl and set aside. Heat the heavy cream until it reaches its boiling point and whisk slowly into the egg mixture. Cook over a double boiler until it starts to thicken. Pour the mixture into ramekins. Set in a water bath and bake for 1 hour. Remove and place in refrigerator for 2-3 hours, or until set.

Sprinkle 1 tbsp. of sugar on top of each brûlée and place under broiler until browned. Serve. *Serves 6.*

CREME FRAICHE

2 cups heavy cream

3 tbsp. cultured buttermilk

Thoroughly combine the heavy cream with the cultured buttermilk and transfer to a covered container. Let sit in a warm place for 8 hours. Refrigerate until ready for use.

Crème fraîche is used on berries and other light desserts. It is often sweetened with sugar and sometimes flavored with vanilla. It is also used unsweetened and unflavored in white fish sauces and curry sauces. *Makes 2 cups.*

CREOLE CREAM CHEESECAKE

GRAHAM CRACKER CRUST

1 lb. graham crackers, crushed   **1 lb. butter**
13 tbsp. sugar

Preheat the oven to 240 degrees. In a 10-inch mixing bowl combine the graham crackers, butter, and sugar. Stir until blended. Press the mixture evenly on the bottom and sides of a greased 10-inch spring-form pan. Set aside.

CREAM CHEESE FILLING

2½ lb. (40 oz.) cream cheese   **3 eggs**
1 cup sugar   **11 oz. Creole cream cheese**

Cream together the cream cheese and sugar with a paddle until smooth. Add the eggs and beat until blended. Add the Creole cream cheese. Beat until thick and smooth. Pour cheese mixture over the crumbs in the springform pan. Bake in the preheated oven for approximately 1 hour and 15 minutes, or until set.

TOPPING

¾ cup sour cream   **2 tbsp. sugar**

Blend together the sour cream and sugar topping and spread topping mixture evenly over the set cheesecake. Place in a 350-degree oven for 5 minutes, or until topping is tacky. Remove from oven. Let cool for 25 minutes in the pan before removing the sides. Cool completely and refrigerate until ready to serve.

GARNISH

Caramel Sauce   **Dark chocolate shavings as gar-**
White chocolate shavings as   **nish**
garnish

To serve the Creole Cream Cheesecake, cut into slices, top with Caramel Sauce, and garnish with white and dark chocolate shavings. *Makes 1 10-inch cake.*

This is also good served with Mocha Sauce.

DESSERT CREPES

1 cup sifted all-purpose flour	**2 cups milk**
1 tbsp. sugar	**1 tsp. vanilla extract**
Pinch salt	**2 tbsp. melted butter**
3 eggs	**4 tbsp. melted butter for the pan**

Combine the flour, sugar, and salt together in a mixing bowl.

In another bowl, beat the eggs together with the milk and vanilla extract. Whisk in the melted butter. Blend the egg mixture into the flour mixture, a little at a time, until all is combined and the resulting batter is smooth. Allow the batter to rest, covered, at room temperature for an hour.

Use a small skillet, 6-8 inches bottom diameter, or a special crêpe pan to make the crêpes. Heat the pan to medium-low heat and pour some of the melted butter in and swirl it around to completely coat the pan's cooking surface. Pour the excess back into the remaining butter.

Now, pour about 2 tablespoons of the crêpe batter into the heated, buttered pan and swirl it around also to completely and evenly coat the bottom of the pan. Cook for about 2 minutes, or until the edges have begun to color and the middle begins to dry. Flip the crêpe and cook for about another minute on the other side.

Slide the cooked crêpe out onto a plate and repeat the process until all the batter is used. Stack the crêpes on top of one another to form a pile. Cover with a cloth and hold until ready for use. *Makes 16-18 crêpes.*

Note: These dessert crêpes can be used in Crêpes Broussard and other fancy crêpe desserts. Or they can be served simply with a little preserves, cane syrup, or honey spread on them, rolled up, and dusted with confectioner's sugar. They are also good with Mocha Sauce.

CREPES BROUSSARD

1 10-oz. package frozen strawberries
¼ cup white sugar
¼ cup water

½ cup strawberry liqueur
12 medium fresh strawberries,
   hulled and halved
12 Dessert Crêpes

Puree the frozen strawberries in a blender. In a saucepan, dissolve the sugar in water and the strawberry puree. Cool for 5 minutes. Add the liqueur and cook until it becomes a thickened sauce. Use fresh strawberries cut in half to enhance the sauce.

Using 12 precooked crêpes, layer them flat on a work surface. Make a filling in the blender using the following ingredients.

FILLING

¾ cup cream cheese
¼ cup whipping cream
2 tbsp. sugar

1 tsp. lemon juice
½ cup chopped walnuts, folded
   in by hand.

Pipe the filling into the crêpes, roll, and heat in the strawberry sauce. Place 2 crêpes per person in a deep dish and serve. *Serves 6.*

FLORENTINE COOKIES

½ cup unsalted butter
1 cup granulated sugar
1 tbsp. honey
½ cup heavy cream
1½ cups chopped pecans

4 tbsp. flour
4 oz. semisweet chocolate
   morsels
2 oz. unsweetened baking
   chocolate

Preheat the oven to 350 degrees.

Combine the butter, sugar, honey, and heavy cream in a saucepan and bring to a boil. Continue cooking until the mixture is golden in color. Remove the saucepan from the heat and fold in the chopped pecans and flour. Drop ½ teaspoonfuls of this mixture 3 inches apart onto a cookie sheet covered with foil, buttered lightly, and dusted with flour. Bake until the edges begin to brown, 8-10 minutes. Remove from oven, cool slightly, and place cookie sheet in the freezer. When cookies are set, they will remove easily from the cookie sheet.

For chocolate coating, gently melt the semisweet chocolate morsels in a saucepan together with the unsweetened baking chocolate. Using a pastry brush, coat the bottom of each cookie with the chocolate and store in the freezer. *Makes 4-5 dozen.*

These cookies are marvelous served alone or as part of other desserts.

FRESH PEAR SORBET AND CHAMPAGNE

1 cup sugar
2 cups water
2 cups pureed fresh pears

¼ cup lemon juice, fresh
1 split champagne (375 ml.)

In a saucepan, over low heat, make a syrup of the sugar and water. Cook only until all granules of the sugar are dissolved.

The pear puree should be made immediately before adding to the syrup so they do not discolor. Add the pear puree to the sugar syrup. Allow the mixture to cool and add the lemon juice.

Process this sorbet mixture in an ice-cream freezer, following the manufacturer's guidelines.

Before serving, place the sorbet in a large chilled silver bowl. Pour the champagne over, and blend with great ceremony. Serve each in a frosted wine glass with a silver spoon. *Serves 6.*

FROZEN POPPY SEED
AND CINNAMON PARFAIT

⅓ cup poppy seeds
⅓ cup milk
4 cinnamon sticks (broken into
    small splinters)
2¼ cups heavy cream

6 egg yolks
3 whole eggs
¾ cup sugar
Praline Sauce
Pecan halves for garnish

Simmer the poppy seeds in milk until almost all of the milk is evaporated, stirring as the mixture becomes thick.

Combine the cinnamon slivers with ⅓ cup of the cream, cover, and cook over low heat for 5 minutes. Remove and allow to steep.

Combine the egg yolks, eggs, and sugar in a heatproof bowl, whisk to blend, then whisk and cook over a pan of hot water until it is thick and shiny with a meringuelike texture. Remove from the heat and whisk over a bowl of cracked ice to cool.

Whip the remaining heavy cream to stiff peaks and fold gently with the egg mixture.

Transfer the poppy seeds to a mixing bowl, stir in a few spoons of the egg mixture to the lighten texture, and then fold in a little less than half of the egg mixture. Strain the cinnamon cream into the remaining unflavored egg mixture and fold to mix well.

Fill six individual molds first with the poppy seed mixture, settle well, then add the cinnamon mixture. Cover and freeze at least six hours.

Dip base of each mold into hot water, run a knife around the edges, and invert onto cold plates. Serve with Praline Sauce and decorate with pecan halves. *Serves 6.*

This is good served with Mocha Sauce.

GRAND MARNIER MOUSSE

6 egg yolks	2 tsp. unflavored gelatin
1½ oz. (3 tbsp.) Grand Marnier	2 cups whipped cream,
6 tbsp. fresh orange juice	unsweetened and whipped
6 tbsp. white wine	stiff
6 tbsp. sugar	

In a large bowl combine the egg yolks, Grand Marnier, orange juice, wine, sugar, and gelatin. Cook over gentle heat until mixture coats a spoon. Refrigerate until cool, fold in the stiff whipped cream, pour into a loaf pan to mold, and chill until set. Serve sliced, scooped into hollowed oranges on crushed ice, or use for Charlotte Russe. *Serves 6.*

GRAND MARNIER SOUFFLE

Butter to coat the soufflé dish	**4 large eggs, separated**
⅓ cup sugar	**Pinch cream of tartar**
½ cup milk	**Pinch salt**
2 tbsp. flour	**2 tbsp. superfine sugar**
2 tbsp. butter	**½ cup Grand Marnier**

Lightly butter a 1½-quart soufflé dish and coat with sugar. Place the dish in refrigerator to chill.

Preheat the oven to 400 degrees.

Pour the milk into a saucepan and sift in the flour, whisking all the while. Bring to a boil and cook until the mixture thickens. Remove the pan from the heat and add the butter, stirring until the butter is melted. Now, whisk the egg yolks into the mixture, one at a time, and hold the pan aside.

In a separate bowl, beat the egg whites until they are foamy. Beat in the cream of tartar and salt. Continue beating until the whites form soft peaks and then add the superfine sugar, a little at a time, until the whites form stiff shiny peaks. Whisk the Grand Marnier into the custard base.

Fold the egg-white meringue into the custard base a third at a time. Pour or spoon this mixture into the chilled mold and place the mold in a "bain-marie," or hot water bath. Place the whole thing into the preheated oven for 10 minutes, then turn the oven down to 375 degrees. Cook for 25 minutes and remove to serve immediately. *Serves 6.*

ISLE FLOTTANTE PRALINE

6 eggs, separated
Pinch cream of tartar
Pinch salt
¾ cup sugar
Butter to grease the mold
6 tbsp. praline, crushed

Water
¼ cup sugar
1 tsp. vanilla extract
1 tbsp. cornstarch
2 cups boiling milk

Separate the eggs and whip the whites in a bowl with the cream of tartar and salt. Whip them until they form soft peaks and add the ¾ cup of sugar, a third at a time, until it is all added. The egg whites, now a "meringue," should now stand in stiff peaks when the whip or beater is removed from them.

Butter a 1½-quart mold and sprinkle with half of the crushed praline. Cover the mold with foil.

In a wide pan, bring 3 inches of water to a boil. Place the mold in the pan, cover the pan, and cook at a very low simmer for about 7 minutes. Remove the mold from the pot, remove the foil from the mold, carefully wrap it with a dry dish towel, cut the top edges of the meringue away from the mold, place a dish on the mold, and flip the whole thing over, shaking it to loosen the meringue onto the plate.

Make the custard by beating the egg yolks together with the ¼cup of sugar until the sugar is dissolved. Add the vanilla and cornstarch and beat in the boiling milk slowly, until it is all incorporated. Pour the custard mixture into a saucepan and return to a low heat. Cook on a low heat while stirring, until the custard has thickened. Do not let the liquid come to a boil; it will separate. Remove the custard from the heat, transfer to a container, cover, and chill in the refrigerator with the meringue.

Serve the dessert by pouring some of the custard onto a dessert plate or bowl, and then a slice of meringue. Sprinkle with more crushed praline. *Serves 6.*

LEMON-TEQUILA SOUFFLE

⅔ cup sugar
1 cup water
6 egg yolks
3 oz. (6 tbsp.) white wine
5 tbsp. lemon juice
1½ oz. (3 tbsp.) tequila

1½ cups whipped cream
6 hollowed-out lemons
Shaved ice
Whipped cream for garnish
6 mint leaves for garnish

Combine the sugar with the water in a saucepan and boil gently until mixture begins to thicken (syrup stage). Remove and let cool thoroughly.

When syrup is cold, combine with the egg yolks, wine, lemon juice, and tequila. Cook this mixture over a low flame, whisking constantly, until the foam goes down. Taste to be sure that the eggs are cooked. Place in the refrigerator and stir occasionally while cooling. When cool, fold in the whipped cream and place in the freezer.

To assemble, spoon the soufflé mixture into the hollowed-out lemons, put on a bed of shaved ice, and freeze. When about to serve, garnish each with whipped cream from a tube and a mint leaf. *Serves 6.*

Try English Tia Maria Cream with this.

POACHED PEARS MADAME PREUSS

⅓ cup raisins
1½ tsp. sugar
3 tbsp. dark rum
6 ripe pears
1½ cups white wine
2 tsp. sugar
1 cinnamon stick

Juice and rind from 1 large
    lemon
⅓ cup water
Raspberry Sauce
6 chocolate cups
1½ cups whipped cream
6 cherries

Preheat the oven to 350 degrees.

Combine the raisins, 1½ teaspoons of sugar, dark rum and hold aside.

Slice the bottoms off the pears. Peel the pears and remove the cores (through the bottom, leaving the stems intact). Stuff the pears with the raisin filling.

Combine the white wine, 2 teaspoons of sugar, lemon juice and rind, cinnamon stick, and water in a large saucepan. Add the stuffed pears, taking care to stand them upright without losing the raisin filling. Poach in the preheated oven for 10 minutes, or until tender.

To assemble the dish, pour a little Raspberry Sauce into the bottoms of six chocolate cups. Top each with a poached pear, stem-side up. Spoon more Raspberry Sauce over the pears. Decorate with whipped cream and cherries. *Serves 6.*

I created this dish for my wife Evelyn, Madame Preuss.

RUMTOFF

2 cups peaches, unpeeled, seeded, and cut into ½-inch cubes

2 cups plums, unpeeled, seeded, and cut into ½-inch cubes

2 cups cantaloupe, unpeeled, seeded, and cut into ½-inch cubes

2 cups pears, unpeeled, seeded, and cut into ½-inch cubes

2 cups raspberries

2 cups strawberries, halved

1 pineapple, peeled, cored, and cut into ½-inch cubes (use last)

Sugar

1 fifth 151 rum

Start Rumtoff in late August as each fruit comes into season.

To make this recipe, you layer a type of fruit, add sugar and rum, and let the layer marinate for 15 days. Your first layer should be the peaches, to which you add sugar (determine the weight of the fruit and add ⅔ as much sugar—if the fruit equals a pound, add ⅔ lb. of sugar). Then cover the layer with 151 rum. Marinate for 15 days. Then add the plums, the corresponding amount of sugar, and 151 rum. Let marinate. And continue this process with the remaining ingredients. Marinate each layer for 15 days before adding the next layer of fruit. Always add the pineapple as the last layer. Rumtoff should be ready 15 days after you added the pineapple, which should put it around Christmastime. Do not use apples, blueberries, or any citrus fruit. Serve over vanilla ice cream. Makes 1 gallon.

SABAYON

8 egg yolks
½ cup sugar
½ cup Marsala wine

1 cup heavy cream, whipped
2 tbsp. Grand Marnier, curaçao,
 or other orange liqueur

Whisk the egg yolks and sugar together in a bowl until they are pale and foamy and the sugar is completely dissolved. Whisk in the Marsala wine.

Pour the mixture into the top of a double boiler and cook while beating constantly until the mixture has thickened and doubled in volume. Turn off the heat and continue beating the Sabayon until it has cooled to near room temperature.

Carefully fold in the whipped cream ⅓ at a time and add the orange liqueur. Spoon into chilled dessert cups or glasses and refrigerate until cold. *Serves 6.*

STRAWBERRY SABAYON

MARINATED STRAWBERRIES

3 cups strawberries, halved
¼ cup kirsch or other cherry
 brandy

2 tbsp. sugar
1 tsp. lemon juice

Combine the strawberries, kirsch, sugar, and lemon juice. Transfer to a covered container and refrigerate until well chilled.

SABAYON

4 egg yolks
¾ cup sugar
¾ cup strawberry liqueur

1 cup heavy cream
½ cup whipped cream

Combine the egg yolks, sugar, and strawberry liqueur in a steel or heat-proof bowl. Cook over moderate heat and whisk constantly until the mixture is slightly thickened. Refrigerate to cool. When the mixture is cooled, stir in the heavy cream and mix well.

To serve, spoon the Marinated Strawberries into glass dessert bowls or wine glasses and nap with the Sabayon. Garnish with a dollop of whipped cream. *Serves 6.*

WHITE CHOCOLATE MOUSSE

4 oz. white chocolate
6 egg yolks
3½ tbsp. sugar

3 tbsp. brandy
1 cup whipped cream

Melt the white chocolate in a small saucepan.

In another saucepan, combine the egg yolks with the sugar and brandy. Cook over low heat and stir constantly until the mixture falls in thick ribbons from your spoon. Remove from the heat and allow the egg mixture to cool slightly, then blend it into the melted chocolate. Cool further and fold in the whipped cream.

Transfer to a covered container and refrigerate until chilled and set. Spoon into glass dessert dishes or glasses to serve. *Serves 6.*

This is good served with Mocha Sauce, Praline Sauce, or Raspberry Sauce.

CARAMEL SAUCE

15 oz. sugar
2 tbsp. light Karo syrup

½ cup cream

Boil the sugar and Karo syrup to an amber color. Blend in cream and allow to cool. *Makes approximately 1¾ cups.*

Use as a topping for Creole Cream Cheesecake and other desserts such as Frozen Poppy Seed and Cinnamon Parfait.

ENGLISH TIA MARIA CREAM

1 cup milk
2 egg yolks
2 tbsp. sugar

1 tbsp. Tia Maria or other
   chocolate liqueur
½ tsp. vanilla extract

Put the milk in a saucepan and bring to a simmer.

Meanwhile, combine the egg yolks and sugar in a mixing bowl, and beat until mixture lightens to a pale yellow color.

Carefully whisk a third of the hot scalded milk into the egg and sugar mixture. Slowly whisk this back into the scalded milk remaining in the saucepan. Continue heating and whisking the custard mixture until it thickens. Strain the custard through a sieve and allow to cool to room temperature. Add the Tia Maria and the vanilla extract.

Serve with Chocolate Terrine, Chocolate Pava, or Lemon-Tequila Soufflé. *Makes approximately 1¼ cups.*

MOCHA SAUCE

½ lb. butter
¼ cup sugar
¼ cup brandy

2 individual pkg. Sanka instant
   coffee
½ pint whipping cream

Combine the butter and sugar in a saucepan and heat and whisk together until the sugar has dissolved. Dissolve the Sanka in the brandy and add it to the warm butter mixture. Remove from the heat and let cool to room temperature. Add the whipping cream to the mixture. Hold sauce at room temperature and don't chill.

Serve with Almond Cookies and Cream Noisette. This sauce is also good with White Chocolate Mousse, Creole Cream Cheesecake, and even vanilla ice cream. Or serve with Bread Pudding, Dessert Crêpes, and Frozen Poppy Seed and Cinnamon Parfait. *Serves 6.*

PISTACHIO SAUCE

1½ cups milk
¾ cup coarsely chopped pis-
    tachios

2 tbsp. sugar
6 egg yolks

Combine the milk, pistachios, and sugar in a saucepan and bring to a boil. Remove from the heat. Beat the egg yolks in a bowl and then slowly whisk in the hot milk-pistachio mixture. Return the liquid to the saucepan and return to a low heat and cook, stirring often, until the mixture begins to thicken. Remove from heat immediately. Transfer to a covered container and refrigerate until ready for use. *Makes 2 cups.*

This sauce can be served either cold or at room temperature. Serve it with Chocolate Salami and other chocolate desserts.

PRALINE SAUCE

1 cup tightly packed dark
    brown sugar
½ cup water
¼ cup light corn syrup

⅛ tsp. salt
½ cup pecan pieces
2 tbsp. butter
½ tsp. vanilla extract

In a heavy saucepan, combine the brown sugar with the water, light corn syrup, and salt. Bring to a boil for 3 minutes and allow the syrup to thicken. Add the pecan pieces and cook for 1-2 minutes more. Remove from the heat and stir in the butter and vanilla extract. Cool to room temperature. Store the Praline Sauce in a tightly capped jar at room temperature. *Makes approximately 1½ cups.*

Praline Sauce can be served with ice cream, White Chocolate Mousse, and Bread Pudding.

RASPBERRY SAUCE

2 cups whole raspberries
1 cup white wine
Juice from 1 lemon
Sugar to taste

1 tbsp. cornstarch mixed with ¼
cup water
2 tbsp. kirsch or other cherry
brandy

In a saucepan, simmer the raspberries, white wine, lemon juice, and sugar for 5 minutes. Whisk in the cornstarch-water mixture and simmer for another 3-4 minutes. Strain the mixture through a sieve and add the cherry brandy. Reserve until ready for use. *Makes approximately 2½ cups.*

Serve with Poached Pears Madame Preuss, Chocolate Pava, White Chocolate Mousse, or vanilla ice cream.

RASPBERRY COULIS

1 pt. fresh raspberries
½ cup sugar

¼ cup water
1 tbsp. arrowroot

Mix the raspberries, sugar, and water together in a bowl. Cover the bowl and allow to sit at room temperature for 2 hours. Puree the raspberry mixture in a blender and pass through a fine sieve or cheesecloth. Reserve ¼ cup of the puree and mix it thoroughly with the arrowroot. Hold aside.

Pour the remaining mixture into a saucepan, bring to a boil, and reduce by a fourth. Whisk in the arrowroot mixture, return to a boil, then remove from the heat. Allow to cool or use hot. *Makes 2 cups.*

Raspberry Coulis is used with both chocolate and vanilla desserts.

RASPBERRY WINE SAUCE

10 oz. fresh raspberries
6 oz. (¾ cup) red Burgundy
  wine
6 oz. (¾ cup) not too dry white
  wine or Sauterne wine

2½ oz. (5 tbsp.) kirsch or other
  cherry brandy
1 cup sugar
3 tbsp. fresh lemon juice
6 tbsp. cornstarch

In a 2-quart saucepan combine the raspberries, red Burgundy wine, white wine, kirsch, sugar, and lemon juice. Over a medium fire bring to a boil. Reduce heat and simmer about 5 minutes.

Dissolve the cornstarch in a little water or wine and whisk into the simmering sauce, then return to a boil. Reduce to a slow boil and cook another 3-4 minutes. Remove from heat and cool slightly.

Strain through a fine strainer or wire-mesh sieve, being sure to extract all liquids from the seeds. Refrigerate and serve chilled. *Makes 2½ cups.*

RUM SAUCE

1 cup water
1 cup sugar
½ cup fruit cocktail
½ cup dark rum
1 tsp. rum extract

A few drops of yellow food
  coloring
2 tbsp. cornstarch, dissolved
  in a little water

In a saucepan combine the water, sugar, fruit cocktail, rum, rum extract, and yellow food coloring. Bring to a boil. Whisk the dissolved cornstarch quickly into the sauce. Bring the sauce back to a boil, lower to a simmer, and cook for 10 minutes or until the sauce has thickened to your desired consistency. Serve hot over Bread Pudding. *Makes about 2½ cups.*

Index